Letters to My Sheep

Teya Brooks Pribac

First published in Australia in 2023
Copyright © Teya Brooks Pribac 2023

www.veganoman.org

All rights reserved. No part of this publication may be reproduced, stored in a retrieval system or communicated in any form or by any means without prior written permission. All requests for reproduction or communication should be made to the copyright holder at pribact@bigpond.com. A catalogue record for this book is available from the National Library of Australia.

ISBN Paperback 978-0-6453747-3-5
ISBN ebook 978-0-6453747-4-2

Designer: Vesna Messec.
Photograph on page 46: © David Brooks.
All other photographs: © Teya Brooks Pribac.

Letters to My Sheep

Teya Brooks Pribac

Contents

Prelude (Note to the reader)	7
Fugue (With J minor)	9
2022	13
2023	107
Requiem and Coda	125
Postscript	131
Endnotes	133
Acknowledgments	134
About the Author	135

Blue Mountains, 22 October 2022

*Prelude
(Note to the reader)*

'Nel mezzo del cammin di nostra vita mi ritrovai…' Halfway through my life I found myself. That's it. I found myself, and the forest around us helped.

Ten years ago, at thirty something, I would probably have felt more like Dante did at the beginning of the Divine Comedy. Lost. But something happened four years ago when I turned forty. I took charge of my life, rather than let it drive me around, and things started to fall into place.

Happiness is not about achieving pleasure, a wise man once said, it's about not being driven by desire.[1] You'll know when you've reached happiness because there will be no need to feel differently, no longing to change the state you're in.

That's where we are now – us and the sheep. This is an assumption, of course. I don't know exactly how the sheep – Henry, Jonathan, Orpheus-Pumpkin and Jason – perceive our life here but they too seem happy, content, a kind of contentment that perhaps can only come with age when the anxious zeal of youth starts to give way to a calmer disposition as one becomes more settled in one's environment and one's skin, if – IF – one is lucky enough to live in a moderately peaceful and safe place, which for a sheep in this world is a miracle rather than the norm.

I'm writing this book because I want people to know that they were here, that we were here, together, and that, at least for a while, it was perfect.

Fugue
(With J minor)

Knock knock... KNOCK KNOCK ... BASH ....BOOOOOOM
Come on! Open up! The others are on their way, they are going to eat all my peanuts if you don't hurry up!

I don't really know what Jason is saying when he is kicking the door to D's writing room but what I imagine he is saying can't be too far from the truth. He doesn't like to compete with others for treats, that's why he often comes to the door by himself. When Jonathan sees his intentions it gives him the idea and he follows, then Henry and finally also Pumpkin. By the time the others have reached the door, Jason has already left, with or without peanuts. He likes being with his sheep companions and doing sheep things together – he is by definition a doer: restless, curious, always ready for action – but he also likes his little intimate moments with the humans when he can feel *special*. It has nothing to do with his size, I think. He's the smallest of the four, while Pumpkin is the largest. Pumpkin also shows the need to feel special. Henry and Jonathan don't, they like their cuddles and their treats but they are not too fussed if they have to share. It could be because Henry and Jonny were raised by sheep rather than humans as in Pumpkin's case and most likely also Jason's. Pumpkin was raised by us – sheep and human – while Jason was found abandoned in a brickyard but he showed clear signs of having lived as a companion to humans.

I have researched in the area of animal studies for over a decade, and have lived closely with sheep for roughly the same timeframe. The evidence is clear: other animals are completely comparable to humans in everything that matters: they have the capacity to experience pain and joy, they love, they grieve, they play, they observe social norms, they help others, they cheat, they think, they believe, they evaluate things, they need the freedom to make decisions about their lives and those of their children, they solve problems, they create them, they can come up with ingenious solutions, they can also sink into despair.

Commonalities of brain/body structure and processes in human and nonhuman animals enable us to predict with high probability what an animal may be feeling in a particular situation. For example, if a sheep loses her child or best friend, her brain will kick-start processes that will lead to the experience of loss and grief, just like human brains do. In terms of quality and intensity of experience, the sheep's grief is completely comparable to the grief of a human.

Details concerning their *thoughts*, on the other hand, are more elusive. It's easier to predict how they feel compared to what they think. When we live with other animals and get to know them better, we can make informed guesses as to what they may be thinking, even in the absence of a common verbal language. The same is true for them: they too learn to guess what our thoughts and intentions may be. Nevertheless, many questions remain unanswered, and a lot of important information uncommunicated.

It's not that I don't try. I talk to them all the time, and they probably talk to me.

Why did you let that dog approach? Couldn't you smell that we were scared?

I know dogs make you uncomfortable but he was lost and we had to look after him.

There's so much I'd like to ask my sheep and so much I'd like to tell them. There are also times when I'm glad I can't.

*

A note on the possessive pronoun in the title: There are many instances where possessive pronouns should be avoided as they reflect an objectifying attitude. Here, however, the 'my' is used in its affectionate capacity, conveying intimacy: they are indeed *my* sheep as much as I am *their* human (or whatever they call me), no sense of possession intended.

2022

1

Three years ago, on this day, Charlie died.

October is a big month for us, isn't it? There's always something major that happens in October. Ten years ago, 2012, it was October when we moved into this place.

A few weeks later Henry and Jonathan joined us. A friend alerted us to a note outside the co-op: someone was trying to rehome two sheep. Sheep? Why not?! We jumped into Vinnie (the old van, named after van Gogh, which we had recently purchased so we could move houses at our own pace) and drove down the mountains to pick them up. That's how it all started. The following year, also in October, Pumpkin joined us, and then Jason just over a year later in early January.

We didn't know anything about sheep when we met Henry and Jonny. I'm sure you two could tell. We couldn't even tell you apart. It's hard to believe it given how distinct your heads and bodies are! But I guess one needs exposure to start noticing, or perhaps to start learning what to look for.

Henry and Jonathan, 2012.

Charlie Dog was sitting in the middle seat between D and me, while the two of you were in the back of Vinnie. By the time we reached home Charlie and Henry had become friends, and remained very close till the end.

I was watching videos this morning of you two playing. It amazes me how smooth the interspecies communication between the two of you was. You were clearly understanding each other's intentions, reading between the lines, so to speak, decoding symbolic gestures – capacities that nonhuman animals are not supposed to have; humans are so full of bullshit, aren't we?

Sometimes you were playing so rough that it was scary: your heads close together, Charlie growling at you with a vicious look on his face, you ready to butt him off the face of the earth. I'd start to get anxious, 'Is this still play?' But you trusted each other fully, and the next thing we know he's licking you affectionately and you're licking him back in a most unsheep-like, dog-like fashion.

Over the last couple of months of his life, Charlie's health deteriorated rapidly, and you were all here witnessing it. I wondered what you saw, what you knew, what you understood, *how* you understood it. What I do know is that you knew he was unwell and that you knew it was serious, and I think you cared.

I know Henry cared. In the last stages Charlie was very weak and he couldn't walk much so I'd often carry him around, remember? One day Charlie was feeling a bit better, Henry noticed it and ran to him. You seemed so happy to have your friend back! You greeted him with a light butt as you would often do in play, but that was too much for poor little Charlie, he was way too weak, and fell over. I think I will always remember that deep sadness and disappointment that I saw on your face:

My friend IS leaving me.

Some say that dogs like to be outside when they are ready to die, Charlie didn't. He insisted on going out onto the lawn for a pee and then he wanted to come into the house. As I was putting you to bed with your hay dinner, Charlie was in his bed with D sitting beside him. Death started knocking.

Charlie, come on, it's time to go.
No, another few minutes, she's on her way.
Charlie, we have to go.
Just a minute, please. Hurry up, T, I'm leaving.

I came back, he passed away a couple of minutes later. Even though ultimately we die alone we seem to like having a caring presence around whether we are dog, human, sheep and possibly anyone else.

2

Three years ago today, we buried him, wrapped in your wool. This was the first time that I buried someone I truly loved. It didn't feel right to just put him in the hole we'd dug for him under the lemon tree. 'Is he going to be cold?' Of course not, he was dead, but I had to make him cosy anyway. Before that, I took his footprints and a bit of fur to make a little 'Charlie's painting' that is now hanging on the wall above his old feeding spot.

It was a challenging day, in all sorts of ways, including your reaction to his dead body.

I wanted you to know that he was dead. I think people – all sorts of people: human people, sheep people, etc. – have the right to know what happens to their friends. I think it's cruel when people just disappear. I try to imagine living in some place controlled by some creatures who couldn't speak my language, like humans can't speak other animals' languages. As a consequence these creatures might think that I was dumb, like humans think of other animals. They'd think that I was unable to capture certain concepts, such as the concept of death, so they wouldn't even try to help me understand what happened to my family and friends, instead they'd simply make them vanish. I wouldn't like that, and I think other animals don't like it either. It introduces a level of uncertainty into the situation that no animal would be comfortable with.

That's why I brought Charlie's body to you. I wanted you to

know. I was holding him in my arms, you came over, looked closely, sniffed him and jumped off. All of you, one by one, did exactly the same thing. I know it was a reaction to his dead body because you'd seen me carrying him around before. Henry and Jonathan often came to say hi to him in my lap and never reacted like this. You smelt death, it must have been the smell.

3

I often wonder how much you know. Humans tend to think of ourselves as the 'knowing animal', partly based on our presumably amazing communicative skills, but there are more things in heaven and earth than are dreamt of by the human. A wealth of senses and agencies to speak to them.

Do you remember that rainy morning when I slipped bringing pellets to you? I wrote about this on a couple of occasions,[2] a memorable fall indeed. The pellets spread all over the place. You gathered around me, and, dutifully ignoring the pellets, you started to sniff in my direction. 'How are you? How is she?' you must have been wondering, as I remained on the ground, immobile, waiting for the acute pain in my leg to subside, and wondering myself: 'How am I? What are you smelling? How much do you know?' How much *do* you know? And how much do you know that I don't?

Some of the most intriguing questions tend to emerge when I find myself – accidentally or intentionally – on the ground. The world looks and feels different on that level. You want to stay there, gripped by the weight of evidence, but you may decide against it, get up, step into the garden (or go for a walk in the woods, or down the street in a big city or a small town, take a dip in the ocean or dig further into the earth), and, like a little Doctor Dolittle, find the world is no longer what it used to be; it is alive and speaking – all of it: that slug crawling along the path is leaving a trail that contains meaningful information for the slug-language-literate, that chirping bird is also saying something that is not just 'chirp-chirp', the grass is singing her own song, the clouds, the pebbles, the wind, and others – all of them, all of us, with our own voices and messages that are meaningful to us and those who can read us.

4

This is freaky! What's this smell?

Smoke? But it's very subtle, maybe there's a fire far away.

What about all these panicky birds suddenly all over the place. Refugees?

Do you think she knows that something is not right? Is that why she's putting the hay into the van?

She's not planning to piss off and leave us here, is she?

She'd never do that! I bet the van is for us.

Yes, we'll all go into Vinnie and off Barcarolle!

Barca- What?

Boat-ing. Offenbach. Beautiful piece. We'll all be safe in Vinnie swinging down some dirt road, as in a boat, toward lush pasture!

Waltzing down the Blue Murray River.

Haha! Cox River more likely.

I'm not sure about boats but pasture sounds good.

Did you know about the fires before the smoke arrived? Did you know how close and big they were? And how many animals lost their homes and lives?

Coincidentally, the fires started on the day Charlie passed away. They grew very quickly and they kept growing. When they eventually died, three months later, they had taken with them three billion native nonhuman animals, and many other nonhuman animals that either don't count because they are considered pests, or count as dollars rather than individuals because they are considered stock: live-stock, including sheep.

'If only we spoke the same language,' I often think. In times like this I'm glad we don't because I might tell you things that you probably don't know and that I hope you never find out.

These fires were unprecedented in size and intensity. The size of our national park exceeds 2.5 million acres, and seventy-nine percent of it was fully or partially burnt. We were right in the middle of two mega-fires. The one to the South was burning four kilometres from us, and the one to the North two kilometres from us. For about two months we were ready to evacuate every day. Vinnie was packed with sheep essentials, the car with human essentials, and our evacuation plans kept changing as the fire was moving around and taking more and more areas.

The odd thing was that for several weeks with the fires burning so close to us, we had virtually no smoke. Sydney was engulfed in a thick cloud of smoke all through that time but the wind direction meant they got it all and we none. I wondered if you knew about the fires during those weeks. Could you smell them? Could you tell something was wrong because there were more cockatoos around than normal? There may have been other things that I didn't notice but you may have? 'Gifted with the extension of the senses we [humans] have lost or never attained, living by voices we shall never hear.' Isn't this passage beautiful? Henry Beston wrote it when he was living alone in a little cottage on a beach.

Anyway, you certainly felt that eeriness in the air that comes with fires and maybe other disasters. Even we, dumb humans, with most of our senses dampened or never developed, can sense that. It's like a choir of all agencies in a particular place vibrating in tune. You can't isolate it through your ears but it's penetrating through every cell.

Then the smoke came to us too, didn't it, and just stayed here. You couldn't remain inside with the doors and windows closed like humans can. And because you couldn't, I didn't feel I could either, in solidarity. It also messed up with my new habit formation plans.

5

Habits – and rituals – are funny things, and you are full of them.

I heard this lovely story the other day: there's a community of rescued sheep (like yourself but more numerous – twenty-nine of them) on the northeast coast of Tasmania. It's a beautiful place, near the ocean, you can literally see the ocean from the paddock – a kind of waterfront with a huge paddock, so perfect! I'm thinking we could move there.

The lovely humans, Paul and Sharon, who look after these fortunate sheep, brought home two huge hay rounds. One hay round contains about twenty square bales that we buy for you. So the rounds are really big! One of the rounds landed on the side instead of vertically and the sheep started to eat into it, virtually turning it into a (cylindrical) donut!

It must have been such fun, and it certainly filled up their tummies! But guess what? At night they lined up for dinner anyway! That's what you do too. You always want your dinner and always want your breakfast, and it's got to be of the right kind: grass pellets for breakfast and Lucerne hay for dinner. If I gave you grass pellets (which you love) for dinner, you'd still line up for Lucerne.

We are all creatures of habit, and that's not necessarily a bad thing. We may develop suboptimal habits, which is going to be damaging in the long run, or helpful good habits. A lot of the time it's really just a matter of stopping and having a look at the habits and where they are likely to take us. If we don't like the direction, we can start working on changing the habits, and the direction too will change.

That's why in July 2019 I started to run first thing in the morning, before coffee, before breakfast, before anything. Start the day on your own terms – don't check your email, don't check the news, don't give in when your sheep realise you're up and *BAAAHHAAAAAAH (!!!!!!)* your head off wanting breakfast. Resist! Ha-ha! Sorry about that, but you adjusted pretty quickly.

Taking a little bit of time in the morning for yourself (a little bit of meditation, exercise, a gratitude session, whatever suits you) adds a protective seal to your day, and you will be better equipped to deal with whatever comes along. If something unpleasant happens in your day, that's all it is: it's not your day (or your life) itself, it's just something that happened *in* your day. Conversely, if you go straight to the email, news, etc. you are making yourself open and vulnerable to whatever hits you from the outside, and the external world eventually ends up controlling your life.

I wonder if sheep have similar experiences. Obviously you don't use technology to displace yourselves like we do, but there may be other ways of being less present than one could be?

We were visiting my parents that July, the route was familiar from my high school running expeditions: up the cemetery hill and then back down via a dirt track with glimpses of the Adriatic Sea. I was only a few months into running when, back here at home, the smoke from the fires reached us. The habit of a morning run was still in the formative phase. It actually took a couple of years to become consolidated. Missing once is okay, but miss twice in a row and you're already starting to form a different habit.[3] What to do? I kept running, with the mask on.

6

This was just before other types of masks became obligatory. If I felt silly running down the street with the mask on during the fires, soon everyone would be walking around (and going to the gym, yoga, shops and everywhere else) masked. Covid-19 spread rapidly. In no time the entire world was in lockdown.

It was the first time that many humans experienced what it was like to be confined to a smaller space with severe restrictions on physical and social activity – something humans readily impose upon other animals as they chain them or lock them up in cages, barns, and aquaria.

Our life hardly changed. We almost felt guilty about how much we enjoyed those two years of isolation. We like being home alone, it boosts creativity. One day I felt like a holiday so I made some Greek food, put on some sirtaki-type music and jokingly posted it on Facebook, tagging Lesbos as my current location.

It was great fun but you looked worried. You always do when I do something out of the ordinary. It must be common for all dependent animals. It doesn't take much to work out what a vulnerable position that is to be in.

What if she's gone mad!? Will we be okay?

Perhaps it was just the music.

Oh no, she's not going to play that stuff every day now, is she?
What the heck is it??
tarraram tarraram tarrarrararam.... tarraram tarraram
tatta–tatta–tatta–tatta..tatatatatatatatatatatata
tatatatatatatatatatatata...tatatatatatatatatatatata
Stop it, Jason!

Sorry, I got carried away... It was kinda cute, jumpy, I actually didn't mind it.

You're very sensitive to music. It's understandable. Music is a powerful emotional agent, it speaks directly to your body and nervous system. It can make you happy, relaxed, or drive you mad. Different types of music will suit different types of moods and situations. Some humans are completely unaware of this, and they impose music and various other sounds and noises upon animals trapped in their living spaces. They think that just because the human likes the sound their companion animals will too, but that's not always the case.

At least here you have space and you can move away from the source if you don't like it, or come close when you do like it. When we play Handel's Largo, for example (without the singers of course!).

Ombra mai fu...Never was a shade so sweet...

And you have plenty of that too here – sweet shade, sweet shelter. Most sheep out there don't. Not even a tree. They live completely exposed to the elements – to

the scorching heat and the freezing cold, the rain, the snow, the hail, the wind.

I can't even begin to imagine what it is like for those without access to shelter given how often you use yours – the trees, your insulated barn, the veranda around it, the carport, the area under the deck – depending on the time of day, weather conditions and other factors.

7

Despite shelter options, and the fact that the land is varied – a paddock, a small forested space, trees to rub against, fences to climb and break through, roses and other forbidden goodies on the other side – I sometimes wonder how good or bad this place is for you. Do you like it? Would you prefer to be somewhere else? With more sheep? With more land? What does it feel like to be in the same, and relatively small, area all your life? If I were to take you on a holiday where would we go? Would you like to go? What would the perfect sheep holiday be like?

There may not be a perfect sheep holiday, there may just be the prefect holiday for a particular sheep. Like there is no perfect human holiday. Some would say going to Paris is a perfect holiday. Definitely not for me. I like going on road trips.

A road trip is probably not the best holiday option for a sheep, unless it's a ride down some dirt track with lush vegetation on the side. You'd love the view and we could stop occasionally for a nibble. But generally speaking roads can be scary for sheep, especially busy ones.

I recall taking Fifi to her new home five hours up north. Remember Fifi from across the valley? And how she cried and cried, alone and miserable, after her daughter's death? She spent her entire life up to that point (about six years) in that quiet paddock surrounded by forest, and one day she finds herself in Vinnie in heavy traffic.

The large window at the back of the van must have created the impression that cars and trucks were about to drive into her. She was clearly uncomfortable but not panicky. It must have taken a huge amount of mental power to work out the nature of the completely novel situation she found herself in, and to establish that it was moderately safe. I was impressed. We stopped half way and shared some biscuits. We were both relieved when we made it there. Her face lit up when she saw other sheep. I stayed in a beach cabin overnight, and had a great trip back in a very smelly Vinnie.

8

Look at this photo of Henry. It was taken on that misty day about a month ago as we were walking on Lynda's side. I showed it to someone at the writers' festival last weekend. She pointed out that Australian forests look different because the leaves grow in clusters at the tips. I'd obviously seen it before but never quite registered it.

We are so lucky to have nice neighbours who let you use their land. Remember when we all got into Vinnie and drove to Ken and the other Linda up the road? Not quite a holiday but a fun trip!

We could probably do more of it, but you get excited and it becomes dangerous. When Pete invited us over to help with the grass a few months ago, I told him it may work once or twice but probably no more than that; we'd been there a few times before he moved in.

People see you quietly grazing and they get a totally wrong impression of you – meek, docile, passive. And it wasn't an impossible proposition, just a matter of opening the side gate and getting you across a dead-end street into his yard. We'd arrange garbage bins so you didn't 'accidentally' end up in the neighbour's vegetable garden (she wouldn't have appreciated it), he was to stand on the side of the street closer to the main road, and jump and wave and look really scary if you headed in that direction, I'd open the gate and run with a bag full of yummy grass pellets, and you'd follow. Because sheep follow.

The first time we made it safely there and back. We had a wonderful time in the lush grass. I was pleased, you were pleased, Pete was pleased. But you didn't really need that grass, you had plenty of food here, so the next outing was going to be all about fun!

Yay we're going again!

Let's not go in this time, let's eat the newly planted little trees near the road!

What a great idea!

Yes! And then let's go eat the neighbour's vegetable garden! There's no fence there.

Exciting!

The neighbour's garden was saved but not much else. Pete jumped, I jumped, and we waved, waved more vigorously, yelled, barked, implored, wept.

I'm just glad we got you all back in one piece.

Sheep follow, of course, but not anyone and not always. The reason sheep follow when sheep do is because sheep are herd animals, like humans.

9

'Herd animals' sounds like an insult, in reality it just means social animals: animals who live in groups, do things together, learn from each other, and develop cultures as a result – human cultures, sheep cultures, kangaroo cultures, cockatoo cultures, and others.

One of the road trips that D and I wanted to do involves Route 66 that goes from Los Angeles to Chicago. The road at one point runs through a beautiful park of petrified trees. There are lots of human visitors to the park and they like to steal pieces of rock even though they know it's illegal. There's actually a sign there advising people not to steal: Don't steal, be a good person, don't be like others! And that's the funny part: a social psychologist turned up and said: Hey, if you want people not to steal the rocks you don't tell them that everyone else is doing it! They can't help themselves; humans tend to instinctually choose what is popular over what is right or otherwise desirable. The psychologist replaced the signs and the level of theft dropped.

All of us social, cultured animals – humans, sheep and others – follow to various extents, it would be silly not to. It's a time saver and often a life saver as well. Imagine finding yourself in a situation when everyone is running panic-stricken in a certain direction. You stop and try to work out what's going on. By the time you do so, you could be eaten by a lion, or, more likely these days, shot by a human gone rogue.

Outside emergencies (and when not on holiday) sheep, humans and other animals may spend a little bit more time evaluating situations, forming opinions and planning actions. For example, in the end D and I decided, for various good reasons, not to give in to our initial impulse to take route 66, but if we had gone, we'd have driven past bighorn territory. Bighorns are a species of sheep. They have horns, like Pumpkin, but much bigger.

Their horns look more like your ancestors' horns, and they are nomads of a sort. They live in the high mountains where the rough and rocky terrain offers protection from predators and cliff overhangs plenty of opportunity for sheltering from the hot desert sun. From there they also enjoy good visibility, which is important for sheep. It helps you detect danger faster but it also feels good and cosy even if you're not in a dangerous place. Visibility has always been vital for sheep as prey animals. As a consequence, after many, many generations of sheep feeling safer in elevated places, all sheep now naturally prefer such places. That's why you always rest at the top of the paddock rather than at the bottom.

Humans can mess with our bodies, and they can try to mess with our heads too, but deep inside we are still the magnificent spirits that have roamed this earth for millions of years, evolved to perfection for the land inhabited and for each other.

So true!

Do you guys know that there are seven species of sheep currently in existence?

I do! I do! The Mountain Sheep, the Bighorn Sheep, the Thinhorn Sheep, The Mouflon who are supposedly our ancestors, the Urial Sheep ... hmmm who else?

The Snow Sheep! Ovis Nivicola from Siberia.

I must have some Nivicola in me. I like snow, it tastes so nice!

There's a subspecies of the Snow Sheep that eats coal!
Weird!
They are a relict subspecies, linked to some ancient sheep that lived thousands of years ago.
And then there's us, Ovis Aries. There are more than 1200 breeds of our species.
Naah! 1200 versions of us?
Yep. But of course all with our own personalities and other distinct features.
Wow! What a gang if we all got together!

In winter the mountaintops get covered in snow and food becomes harder to access. The bighorn herd will have to decide whether to stay and risk starvation or move to lower ranges and become vulnerable to predation. These are hard decisions that sheep make after careful consideration of environmental and other factors. It's not an impulse and it's certainly not instinctual and automatic. *Does it look like there's good vegetation down there? Have you noticed many mountain lions recently? I wonder if that old shelter we used in the past is still available.*

Past experience and memory play a critical role in these migrations, as does cultural transmission of knowledge – stuff we learn from others in our community: parents, friends, etc. Elders (in sheep and other species) possess useful knowledge that can save the entire herd: for example, they may remember some old source of water in a time of drought. If a herd of sheep is forcibly translocated to a new territory, they are not going to migrate. It will take them several generations to acquire enough knowledge of the new area and growth cycles of the plants to feel safe enough to move around again.

It's taken humans a while to recognise the existence of culture in sheep and other nonhuman animals. It's now widely accepted that there are two types of evolution and inheritance systems in the animal realm: the genetic inheritance system, which determines our species, the colour of our hair, eyes, whether we prefer to sleep in elevated areas with grand views (like sheep) or hidden away in underground tunnels like prairie dogs, and many other features and behaviours. Then there's the cultural inheritance system that is based on the transmission of knowledge among members of a group and across generations.

10

A lot of what animals (sheep, humans and others) do, think and feel is influenced by culture. We are who we are in large part because of our relations with others. There's a pretty straightforward explanation for this.

When we are born (or hatched, if we are birds or some other animals) our brain is not fully developed yet. The rest of the body and all the systems within the body also still need to mature. All these systems develop under the influence of our immediate environment – our parents, siblings and other animals around us, but also the space in which we are being raised – is it noisy, quiet, calm, frantic? All this will affect how our organism develops physiologically and neurologically (how we respond to stress, whether we are more or less prone to inflammation, and other things) but also ideologically (our perceptions and values).

As far as physiology/neurology is concerned, the story goes: if a lamb, a chick, a human baby or some other infant becomes upset the parent will (hopefully) try to calm the infant down. The parent can be a biological parent but they can also be a foster parent or an adoptive parent, it doesn't really matter – even the species of the parent doesn't really matter – as long as there's a moderately mature and competent person there who tries to look after the infant.

If this adult/parent is able to soothe the infant every time the infant gets upset, the infant's system, which is still developing as we said earlier, will start to get the idea that getting upset is normal but that it's also something that one can quite easily overcome and be happy again.

If, on the other hand, the adult/parent is not able to soothe the infant in distress (and this doesn't mean that they haven't tried soothing!), the infant's system will learn that stress is this huge awful monster that is going to devour me and there's nothing I can do about it!

That's how we end up with people – human people, sheep people and people of other species – who handle

stress really well, they know it's unavoidable but they also know that there are ways to work with it and get over it. Then we also have people – humans, sheep, crocodiles and others – who in a stressful situation become completely overwhelmed, and they have no clue as to how to cope with it. With repetition this leads to chronic stress and other related conditions that affect the physical and psychological health of individuals.

Humans know this is true for humans, but they often fail to appreciate that the same processes determine psychological and physical vulnerability or resilience of other animals too. Humans fail to recognise that other animals' psyche is completely comparable to humans' psyche. Nonhuman animals are not automatons; what a nonhuman animal experiences in the early developmental period and then all through lifetime will mark the nonhuman animal just like it marks the human animal.

That's why I freaked out when Sy brought Pumpkin here as a tiny baby. I had just learnt about all this and I was very aware how badly I could damage you! I also knew that my good intentions counted a bit, but in the end it was going to be my own anxiety levels, capacity to cope with stress, and similar factors not entirely in my control that will transfer on to you and determine your own capacity to self-regulate and deal with the ups and downs of life. The least I could do was to try to act like a mother sheep would – be there with you and for you when you needed me, and trust that Henry and Jonathan would do their bit.

Do you remember when I first put that plank down so we could walk across the creek instead of having to jump? Henry and

Jonny would not go near it. You both happily followed me when I carried goodies or when I took you for (what you deemed to be) a 'safe' walking expedition but you weren't going to step onto that plank. Then Pumpkin arrived and he followed me across no problem because he was a baby and I was his mum. And you followed him. I wondered why. He was a baby; in all other circumstances he followed you, you didn't follow him. Then I thought it was probably that once you saw a set of hooves (Pumpkin's) managing the plank without slipping you felt more comfortable trying it. And we've used it ever since. So yes, sheep follow when they decide it's wise to do so.

11

In the French language the first person singular form of the verbs *to be* and *to follow* is identical: *je suis* = I am; *je suis* = I follow. I find it beautiful because it expresses so clearly the biological, psychological and social/cultural process of becoming *me*.

Humans are quick to condemn sheep as 'stupid' for being 'followers' without recognising the extent to which our own being and behaviour are impregnated with social learning, imitation and other forms of dependency on people around us. These things influence our feelings as well as our decision-making.

For example, the reason humans talk about sheep as 'stupid followers' is because these humans heard it from other humans. Most of them have never met a sheep, let alone lived with one, and most haven't read sound ethological work on sheep either. They've adopted this myth by imitating others and learning from them, essentially *following* their lead.

When we are little, this kind of following makes sense. We just got here, we don't know much about the world so we listen to our parents and others with more experience. We learn what we should do, what we shouldn't do, what to eat, what not to eat, how to use this tool or that, and many, many other things. Some are more useful than others, and some are plain wrong, but because we learned them so early on, before we had the capacity to evaluate the pieces of information fed to us, they have entered our kitty of valued assumptions, of what we assume to be 'truths' about the world, and we rarely stop to question them. This is how unflattering myths about sheep, among other things, propagate. This is what we call cultural inheritance and it affects everyone, including scientists.

Until recently, in fact, sheep didn't get much scientific attention because, well… sheep are not interesting, right? Wrong. It's because human scientists thought so because that's what their society had taught them. If no one studies sheep there won't be any evidence to dispel the myths of sheep being stupid etc. Without such evidence, the myths continue.

Science is objective but only to a certain extent. Emotions and culturally transmitted values play an important role in what we look for and what we find.

For example, when we are designing experiments to test nonhuman animals' emotional and cognitive capacities we first have to choose which species we are going to test. This means that some other species doesn't get tested, and as a consequence there won't be any evidence in this second species of whatever we are looking for in the first one (unless someone else decides to test this other species).

Another problem could be finding ways to communicate the research question to the species/individual tested, because obviously we can't just ask using human language. We have to devise clever ways of asking and making sure the tested subject understands. Sometimes we succeed, other times we don't. In the latter case we end up with *no* evidence for that particular thing in that particular species, not because *you* (the tested nonhumans) failed but because we (the testing humans) failed.

Another important aspect is the complexity of the question: are we asking complex questions or simple ones? And why? Do we assume that there is no complexity that we could possibly find in a specific species? This has often been the case. Scientists assumed that sheep weren't complex so they didn't design experiments that would look for complexity in sheep. But they designed such experiments for primates because the scientists believed that primates *were* complex. As a consequence we ended up with mountains of evidence for primate complexity and none for the complexity of sheep – not because sheep are not complex but because no one bothered to get the evidence. Once they started to look into sheep complexity – Taadaaaa! It was all there.

Geez! Humans are so dumb! Complex yes, but also dumb.
 Tell me about it…
 I think the coolest thing about sheep is that we can see behind us without turning our heads!
 I think it's cool that we can just smell each other and know exactly how the other is feeling. I've heard that humans have to tell each other, and then they lie about it and complicate their lives for no reason.

We also know how others are feeling if we just look at their faces and even photos of their faces!

Yes, and we recognise individuals in photos at different ages and face orientations.

Humans still have to work out how to test us for mirror recognition.

What's that?

Humans have this little obsession with mirrors, a bit like Jason: 'Oh, I'm soooo beautiful! I can't stop looking at myself when T puts the mirror out.'

You are just jealous...

Anyway, the humans keep testing other species trying to work out if we can recognise ourselves in the mirror. They think that if we can recognise ourselves in the mirror it's a sign that we are self-aware, and that if we can't we are not self-aware.

Of course we are self-aware!

Of course, but humans haven't worked out how to read us yet.

12

You have these little intimate moments, like the one yesterday on our evening walk: Jason and Jonathan grazing really close together, your bodies parallel, almost touching but not quite. (I wonder if the tips of your wool *were* actually coming in contact in places. The tips are very sensitive, I can hover over your back with my hand and as soon as I touch the tips ever-so gently, you twitch. The power of hair!) Suddenly Jason butts Jonny on the side of the body, quickly and lightly, as you do when you want to show playful affection, and then again, an even quicker butt this time, and you both peed and continued to graze close together. It took me a while to realise that peeing is another sign of happiness in sheep, a bit like a smile in humans.

13

Have I told you about the magic detection project that I've started recently? It's a photographic project documenting nature's magic around us. I'm collecting old images I had taken of the skies,

of the land and everything in between, in a special folder. I'll be adding new ones to it, too. So much one finds if one looks. Like these crystal formations on the front steps one winter morning.

Summer has its magic too, as do other seasons. Humans are surprised when I tell them that they can make their own rainbow, or that *we* can: on a late summer afternoon, stand in the middle of the paddock, facing east with the sun behind you, and swivel the water hose in front of you to create a perfect rainbow circle, over and over again.

The purpose of the magic-detection project is to cultivate greater sensitivity to the world around me, and to encourage other humans to do the same, so that together we can preserve what still can be preserved. Not only for human posterity. It's not all about us, I tell them.

Some moments of magic can't be captured with the camera, like the intimate transactions between Jason and Jonny. One can get the visuals right, but not the essence. One has to be present, and feel it.

14

The Pumpkin & Cook encounter at the 2013 *Nup to the Cup* was also one of those moments.

Nup to the Cup is essentially a protest against the huge horse race known as the *Melbourne Cup*, but we preferred to think of it as a celebration of horses (and all other animals) who shouldn't be used for human entertainment (or any other purpose). Do you know that a horse dies every 2.5 days on Australian racetracks? Crazy. We started the *Nup to the Cup* (then known as the *Not the Cup*) events in 2011 at the University of Sydney. The idea quickly took off and similar events are now being organised all over Australia every year.

The other day I was going through old photos and came across those from past events, including some featuring baby Pumpkin. You probably don't remember, you were very young, about a month old. We couldn't leave you alone here with your uncles – Henry and Jonathan – all afternoon, we didn't trust them enough. So we put a dog harness on you, packed some milk and poo bags, and took you with us. I expected you to lie down in the car and go to sleep like dogs tend to, but you didn't. You stood up the entire trip, looking out intrigued. Unsurprisingly, you turned into a bit of a celebrity among the attendees. Humans don't see lambs very often, at least not live ones.

The event took place at a restaurant on campus. It had a lovely courtyard so we stayed there. At some point the cook came out. Apparently she'd heard about you. She went down to her knees to be at your level and she started to weep. She wept for a while, then she left, without a word to anyone.

It reminded me of a story from Edgar's Mission Farm Sanctuary. They had a stall at a nearby market, as sanctuaries often do. They had a young pig with them. It helps to show humans that other animals are *real* beings, not just numbers or pieces of flesh. A man came past, he stopped, knelt down with the pig and started to weep. He wept and wept, and as he was weeping he kept saying: 'what we used to do to you... I am so sorry... what we used to do to you...' The man had been a slaughterhouse worker.

Out of sight, out of mind.

15

Slaughter used to take place in towns and cities, in front of everyone. It is no wonder that humans protested. Some humans protested the abuse and slaughter themselves – there was a strong vegetarian movement in the 19th century in Europe, Britain, USA and Australia, perhaps elsewhere in the world, too. Others only protested the sights, the sounds and the smells of suffering animals – too hard to bear so they demanded slaughter be removed from view. So it was – to city fringes first, then further away, to the point that nowadays humans can't see what goes on inside slaughterhouses even if they want to. Usually they don't want to.

Some have to. The humans who work there. Most humans don't want to work there. The reason they end up there is because they have very few employment options. Slaughterhouse management often takes advantage of their situation. Sometimes a brave journalist (there aren't many brave journalists around) will tell the workers' stories. Horrific stories. Workers are often made to work for long hours without breaks, they may be forced to wear diapers or resist drinking water for the entire duration of the shift, which can go on for twelve hours seven days a week.

The rule of thumb in a slaughterhouse is that *the line never stops*. Whatever happens, work goes on. Nonhuman animals' suffering doesn't matter, nor do human workers' needs and injuries. 'I've seen bleeders, and they're gushing because they got hit right in the vein, and I mean they're almost passing out, and here comes the supply guy again, with the bleach, to clean the blood off the floor, but the chain never stops,' one worker explained.[4] Human Rights Watch[5] reports that human rights violations in these workplaces are not lapses, they are part of the job, and if a slaughterhouse wanted to improve conditions for the workers, it would become uncompetitive. So conditions don't improve.

Death is never pretty, I once heard a farmer say. Some deaths are less pretty than others. Nonhuman animal suffering is endemic in the slaughterhouse – humans can rest assured that every animal killed in that place has suffered. All farmed animals, not only those farmed for their flesh, end up in the slaughterhouse.

Sometimes a recording gets released showing 'extreme' cruelty to nonhuman animals on their way to death, that is to say, a human worker is being recorded intentionally abusing nonhuman animals more than is required for the purpose of killing. On the rare occasion such recordings reach the human public, the public tends to think of this abusive human as a 'bad apple', 'subhuman' because 'humans don't behave like this'. Don't we?

I have come to believe that those who abuse the most are actually hurting the most; that they need to devalue, in their minds, even further the animals they are about to kill, strip these animals of any worth, so they can kill them in the first place.

Hmm, not a letter to send to you, is it?

16

Are you toilet-trained, Jason?

One of the reasons we've never adopted another dog after Charlie's death has been the pronounced change in dynamics. Henry and Jonathan have remained pretty much the same; the two of you probably miss Charlie and perhaps wouldn't mind another dog provided they were equally eager to groom you. But Pumpkin and Jason have changed quite a bit. It's as if Charlie's presence was holding you back. Is it because you were both raised by humans and you feel there should be a direct relationship between you and the human without a dog who is always following the human, living in the house with the human, even trying to help the human 'control' you? Not that I ever asked Charlie to control you but he did – he tried to predict what I wanted and then implement it. He was mostly right, such as when he tried to prevent you from destroying some plant, but it annoyed you anyway.

With Charlie gone, Jason now follows me around. You want to be part of everything. When I was renovating the cabin kitchen you were constantly at the door, examining the development, smelling newly introduced objects, a bit like a companion dog would. You seem to have adopted the cabin kitchen as 'your' room, the way D's study is Pumpkin's room because he spent a lot of time there as a baby watching the big boys through the window.

You've never peed inside. Were you toilet-trained?

I remember Pumpkin going into 'your' kitchen once. I was outside and I didn't see what he was doing, but he spent a bit of time in there before leaving. You weren't around so you didn't see any of this, but you turned up soon after, you went into the kitchen and ran out immediately with a very worried look on your face.

Oh no! Pumpkin peed in the middle of the kitchen and now she'll think it was me!! Her sense of smell sucks, she'll never know it was Pump!

It was so unusual that I had to check what was in there, and I found a pool of pee on the floor. You didn't have time to produce the pee, it must have been Pumpkin. When you saw it, you left immediately so I wouldn't think it was you. I can't know for sure, but I'm pretty certain that's what happened.

17

Pumpkin also changed after Charlie's passing. You've turned into a true leader. I'm sometimes surprised at your emotional intelligence. Jason would probably beat you in some conventional cognitive test but you'd definitely excel in more holistic evaluations.

I first noticed it when Pixie was here a few years ago. Do you remember Pixie, the tiny sheep? She was an adult but very small, even smaller than Bessy whom we rescued the year before that. Pixie also ended up on the central coast, like Fifi did, but Pixie was small enough to fit into the car.

I don't know where Jason learnt that sort of stuff – maybe by watching the rams down in the valley while they were still there – but he started to harass Pixie immediately and tried to mount her. Pixie managed to get away from him and to the top area, and you Pump blocked the little gate so no one could go through. You'd never done that before. You often stand at the gate, facing the gate, so there's enough space for them to push past you if they want to. They normally don't, I suspect out of respect (or is it fear?) for your horns, but this time you were standing across, blocking the opening completely. Until I came to Pixie's rescue.

This was the first of the many occasions I've noticed you take charge of stuff that Charlie would have tried to look after. I don't know what went wrong with the relationship between you and Charlie. You played with him when you were little and he gave you tonnes of kisses but then it all stopped. I don't think there was any animosity involved, you seemed to have come to an agreement, for some reason, to stay out of each other's life.

Aren't relationships complicated!

18

Some are complicated, others are simply sweet. Such as your relationship with the wild rabbit. I miss seeing him cross the road in the morning when I return from my run. But more than that, I miss watching him play with you, especially Jason. You and the rabbit had a very special relationship, didn't you? He'd be around most of the night, lying with you, running around you in play, going up on his hind legs and grooming your nose and head with his little front paws. He'd then go off to the others for a little while and always come back to you. I sometimes feel guilty for invading your privacy through the cameras (which we've installed for your safety, not for voyeuristic purposes!) but we'd miss so much of your life without them.

D assumed the rabbit lived under his writing room, and that the entrance to his quarters was near the water tank where Pumpkin usually sleeps. But why would he leave in the morning? Was it to avoid us humans?

Free-living animals are becoming increasingly more nocturnal. Humans are everywhere, even a seemingly innocent activity such as hiking is an intrusion into their homes and a disruption of their life; it represents a possible danger so they have to stop whatever they are doing and attend to the invader(s). With so many humans all over the place it is becoming difficult for free-living animals to avoid us in space, that's why they have started to avoid us in time – by becoming nocturnal, by limiting their activity in daylight and increasing it at night.[6] Perhaps the rabbit was trying to evade the fox who lived in the forest area and in the end probably killed him.

19

Did you see the fox kill the rabbit? I often wonder how much you've seen, how much you've actually experienced in your life. Ten years (on average for all of you) is quite a long period, and so much happens, even in this little paddock. Then you'd be seeing things happening down in the valley, things that humans, distracted by our virtual worlds, often miss, but you don't.

Do you know all the animals who live here or visit? I know you know the foxes. Sometimes you'd be lying down relaxing or quietly grazing, a fox would walk right past you and there'd be absolutely no reaction. Once I even saw Jonathan following a fox, and the fox looked a bit concerned and left. I think this means you know the fox and you know s/he is not going to hurt you. Other times a fox appears in the paddock and you become alarmed. This used to signal a new fox, one that you didn't know. But things have changed since Lynda got the hens.

Foxes have killed several of them, and I know you've witnessed some of the killings. Now you become alarmed every time you see a fox. And so do others around here.

I can usually tell when a fox is present because all the birds – especially the magpies – start calling and swooping, and you too go on alert. Everyone watches everyone and quickly learns to read and interpret calls and behaviours. When I see this, I look across the fence and sure enough there'll be a fox near the chicken coop. Except for once. Do you remember when the Indian mynahs were still coming to nest in the cabin's roof in springtime? And that day when they went berserk? You were all spooked, and so must have been the poor young brown snake who had, as I later realised, caused the alarm in the first place. The mynahs chased her all the way down to the end of the paddock and would not stop until she was off the periphery.

Such a delicate and beautifully interconnected world out there. Every move, every sound, every smell is worth a thousand human words.

20

Humans have very little respect for this world. We have failed so badly.

Do you know that, measured in biomass (which means: the total quantity or weight of organisms), of all the mammals on this planet, only five percent are wild, free-living animals, thirty-six percent are humans and fifty-nine percent are so-called farmed animals? And of all birdlife, only a third are wild birds, the rest are 'farmed' birds – chickens, turkeys, and others, enslaved for human greed.

The entire planet has been adapted to serve the human species – so many lives lost and resources used for a species that doesn't even want to be here, doesn't know *how* to be here and be happy, doesn't try very hard, does all it can to escape this world.

The metaverse – a 3D virtual world – apparently already has 400 million monthly active users, and the number is growing. So far these users have purchased over US$500 million worth of virtual real estate[7] (cheap property that doesn't exist). In the metaverse you can buy virtual land, you can buy a virtual house to put on this land, you can probably also buy a virtual creek, a forest, maybe even some virtual extinct animal, virtual cars, virtual clothes, virtually everything. Then what?

21

The main problem with consumerism is that it makes humans unhappy. Unhappy humans tend to spread their unhappiness around and make others unhappy, including nonhumans.

I once read that the recipe for happiness is very simple. It's just a matter of not wanting what you don't have. Of course everyone – humans, sheep and others – needs food and shelter, but true essentials aside, a lot of what we think we need we don't really need. It takes a bit of time and training to work out what those things that we think we need but don't really need are. The best way to start this process is to begin noticing what we *do* have (instead of focusing on what we *don't* have, which a lot of humans do) and being grateful for the things we have:

Can I turn the tap on and out comes clean water? Do I have food in the fridge? Do I have a roof above my head? Small things that are not so small after all – a lot of humans and other animals don't have them. If we focus on what we have we soon start feeling lucky and wealthy.

If on the other hand I keep focusing on what I don't have, I will probably never have enough, regardless of how much I actually have. My mindset will be one of wanting, and wanting more. I end up living in a constant state of needing (rather than *having*). In the state of constant needing I am never enough, never complete, always lacking, in need of more, dependent on what *is not* here rather than what *is*.

As we become increasingly dependent on external 'regulators' (those external things we reach for in order to momentarily fill the gap, such as purchasing goods we don't need, binging on this-and-that: from TV shows to alcohol, cakes and others), our internal system of self-regulation starts to weaken. Our body has the capacity to regulate itself in all sorts of ways, but it's like a muscle, the more we use it the stronger it becomes, and vice versa. Once we lose the capacity to self-regulate unpleasant internal states, we lose a huge amount of power over our own lives and happiness.

This is not just a human thing, it can happen to sheep too. We are talking about very basic mechanisms that we all share. If you become used to constant treats in the form of grass pellets, wheat bars or other stuff that you like, you'll want more and more, and you'll never be happy again.

That's why I try hard not to spoil you.

22

Okay, you are a little spoilt but not to the extent that could hurt you. It's a difficult balance to try to work out in captivity. You are deprived of so many freedoms, what right do I have to impose more restrictions upon you? The honest answer is: I have zero rights, and in a less imperfect world you'd be free to come and go as (and *if*) you pleased.

Ironically, in captivity, it's these further restrictions that make life more bearable, even interesting. For example, if I gave you

24/7 access to the grass pellets that you love and that we now use as a treat, you'd soon stop appreciating them the way you do now, and essentially you'd be left without treats. Unless I came up with some other idea for a treat, but that too could only work if I limit access. I think you know all this, that's why you don't push too much.

A lot of the time it appears to be less about the food and the flavour and more about the act itself, a ritual that you've established and that means something to you. It was pretty clear when you rejected peanuts from Katy. *They rejected peanuts??* We couldn't believe it. We left her with a bag full of peanuts so she could bring you some every day when she came to poop-scoop last time we were away. We were thinking that you'd miss peanuts given that you knock on D's door every day demanding some. But no, it wasn't about peanuts, it was about something else.

What is Aunty Wheat-bars doing bringing us peanuts?!

You looked disappointed, she said, even insulted, when she turned up with peanuts. So she shifted back to the cereal bars, resetting sheep happiness. Sometimes you are pretty easy to read without verbal signs! And aren't you lucky that we are so attuned?! Or at least trying to be.

I wonder if you know how much our life actually revolves around you, and that you pretty much run this place. The entire property is adjusted to you, to *us* living here together. I think you do know. You must know, especially when you look at those poor sheep down at the bottom and realise how *nothing* is adjusted to them.

I would protect you with my own life. I mean this. If we found ourselves in a situation of danger – be it a threat of human violence or a natural or other disaster – and I survived without having done all I could to save you, I don't think I could live with it. The thought, the memory, the image of your dying faces asking

Why aren't you doing something?
would haunt me for the rest of my life.

23

Just like certain images haunt me now.

We live in a bubble. There's no denying it. The world out there is not a nice place. We hide away here where we have everything we need: food, shelter, space, each other, play, freedom from pain, we can see the stars and we smell the seasons as they come and go. It's not one-hundred-percent safe, no place in this world is, but perhaps it is nearly as good as it gets. Sometimes we forget – I forget – that this is *our* world, it's not *the* world. Then I go out or something reaches in from outside, and the bubble bursts (again).

I try not to watch exposés of cruelty to nonhuman animals because the images stay with me, I can't get them out of my head, but sometimes I force myself to watch out of solidarity for the courageous human witnesses who exposed the cruelty and for the innocent nonhuman victims who suffered it. This is how I ended up watching a program on live export. And that's when I saw that face that I'll never forget. A young merino boy, half buried in excrements that no one was going to clean for weeks to come, looking straight into the camera panting as he was cooking inside out. Literally, the vets explained.

He looked so much like Pumpkin. He was Pumpkin. A someone, not a something. A pulsing, feeling, psychologically, biologically and socially complex individual, comparable to us in all that matters.

The lack of space, starvation, exhaustion, heat, injuries, they are 'fighting for their lives, unaware of the hell that still awaits them' if they survive the journey, said a vet on-board of
several of these death ships.[8] Many lambs are born on-board. Instead of soft grass and a happy mum to lick you clean, as nature wanted it, imagine being born into a pile of shit. Another image haunting me.

This is where politicians lose all my respect. Left, right. They do nothing. Ever. Sheep and other farm animals are virtually without protection. Anything can be done to you if deemed 'necessary', and 'necessary' is a euphemism for 'profit'.

One can point this out to politicians, and they will take more or less notice depending on how close the elections are. 'Did you hear that?' I want to grab them by the shoulders and shake them back to sense and sensibility. 'Did you register it? Are you still able to care?'

Are they?

24

On land it's not much better. 'Sheep are tough,' they say. They trap you in barren paddocks with no shelter and oftentimes no food or even water. Dust bowls. And it's perfectly legal. You may freeze in winter and burn in summer. Legal. They can intentionally keep you undernourished so you produce finer wool. They can shear you just before winter so they can sell your wool twice – summer and winter. If they enslave you for your flesh, they may shear you before winter so you eat more and grow fatter. They cut parts of your body off for their convenience. All legal.

Then I see you, protecting your bodies and nurturing your aches and wounds, like humans do our own. I remember a shearer once being surprised at the softness of your skin. He'd never seen anything like that before. He put it down to a good life and the mineral block (which also surprised him, 'you don't often encounter those', he said). I see you running for shelter when it starts to rain, and think of all those who can't. I see you burying yourself into the warm straw in the barn when temperatures drop, hiding in the cool under the deck when temperatures soar, rubbing your bodies against trees and structures when you feel like a scratch or want to mark something with your smell, and many other things that you do, that sheep do, or should be able to do but often can't.

I see them in you, and you in them. These are the moments when I'm grateful (or hopeful) that you can't read my mind because sharing the pain in this case wouldn't halve it, quite the opposite.

25

Who has the prettiest-est-est curls in the entire universe?
I do!
You do indeed, Jason. But they are getting a bit long, let's trim them!
No!
Get Jason!
Stay away from me!
Run, Jason, run!
Get off me! My curls are precious!
Figaro qua, Figaro là…
Heeeeeelp!

Jason was named after a human Jason with similar curls and a slightly different temperament.

They must keep you warm even though they are very light, especially compared to Pumpkin's. Pumpkin's wool is thick and heavy. He is a merino, a 'wool sheep', bred to produce excessive amounts of wool to keep humans cosy and sheep miserable. His skin is more wrinkled compared to others so it can grow more wool, it's also more likely to get cut during shearing. The weight of wool can kill a sheep. If they accidentally roll on their back they may not be able to pull themselves back up. The heavy wool keeps them down and their often undernourished bodies struggle in vain. They die there, on their back, out of stress. That's how Pumpkin's mum died in early October 2013. You were found lying beside her motionless body when you were only a few days old.

One day two years ago, in late spring when your wool is heaviest, you also rolled on your back. I was inside and I heard you calling, then Jason started to call. It all sounded very urgent. I came out and you were on your back, in the small depression you'd dug under the deck to make your sleep more comfortable, unable to get up. I'll never forget the fear on your face.

I wonder what would have happened to you had your mother not died? Would they have used you to show the students how to exsanguinate a sheep? You were at a university farm after all, and a disposable subject. Exsanguination (cutting into your flesh and letting you slowly die by bleeding out) is supposed to be banned in vet classes but that didn't stop the professor from doing it to some other sheep. Sy, your rescuer, who was a student at the time, complained to the faculty but I'm not sure much happened to that stick-in-the-mud.

Exsanguination or perhaps even something worse. I'm so glad we got you out of there.

26

Bubbles are not necessarily a bad thing. Yes, they can burst, but they also give us hope and show us how things could be.

A wise human named Stephen[9] came up with the principle of two circles of action/reaction: the circle of concern and the circle of influence. The circle of concern includes all the things that we care about. It can be big or small, depending on how many things we care about. In this circle there are some things we can do something about and other things we can't do much or anything about. Within the circle of concern there's another circle – the circle of influence: this circle includes things that we care about and *can do* something about.

Stephen's idea – and it makes sense to me – is that when one focuses on, and works in, the circle of influence this circle begins to expand, taking more and more space inside the circle of concern. As this happens, the circle of concern naturally begins to shrink. In other words, the more we focus on the circle of influence the more our influence on things that matter to us grows. And the other way around: if we become too preoccupied with the circle of concern and don't do enough within the circle of influence we may find that the circle of concern begins to expand, and, in the process, it shrinks the circle of influence. Our influence in things that matter to us diminishes, and we may become overwhelmed or even break.

Human activists helping abused animals or advocating for them face continuous failures by authorities to protect these victims, and as a consequence these activists are particularly at risk of becoming overwhelmed and burning out.

I see our bubbly life here as strengthening our circle of influence. It keeps us focused on what we can do rather than what we can't do. For example, it gives me the opportunity to get to know you and talk about you to other humans. This exposes those humans to notions of sheep that they might otherwise not have encountered, and this may change how they think and eventually how they act.

It exposes *me* to notions that I myself would likely have missed. I turned vegan overnight when someone pointed out to me that I was personally responsible for the horror other animals endure. Through my food and other choices I was

pouring money into an industry that tortures and kills sentient beings. The way out was easy, they said: stop buying those products. So I did, the easiest thing I've ever done, and I felt happy, light and free.

For a long time my activism revolved around pain. Then you came into my life and my world turned upside down (in a good way!)

*'Listen to me and you shall hear, news hath not been this thousand year
  Old Christmas is kickt out of town
  Likewise then did die rost beef, mutton and shred pie
  With plant-based goodies on the rise our friends will stay alive, and
  We'll all be content, not just the human kind, in this world turned
upside down.'*

*You are a true poet, Jonny!
  I'll happily march to that! Jingle bells no more chopped tails!*

Pain is hugely important and something to avoid inflicting upon others if we can, but focusing on pain somehow obscures capacities and potentials that make you – sheep and other nonhuman animals – completely comparable in your complexity to humans.

It also creates the impression that if we somehow managed to avoid inflicting pain it would be okay to enslave you and use you for our purposes. But that is never okay because as soon as we give ourselves the right to 'own' someone, we take that someone's self-determination away. And while you may want to avoid pain – of course, all animals do – you don't want to give up your freedom, the freedom to make decisions about your own life and create heaps of opportunity to feel good, great and awesome!

When I started to live with you I started to see things I could not have known before. As a consequence, the violence and deprivation that humans impose upon sheep and other animals has become even more pronounced and harder to tolerate.

27

One of the fascinating things about living with sheep is that we come in contact with humans whom we'd otherwise probably never know, such as farmers and shearers. They are weird folks, there's lots of negotiating they do internally. Though not all of them probably. Jack's wife, for example, didn't seem to have any ethical problem whatsoever with what they were doing – breeding 'meat' sheep commercially and some 'poultry' for personal consumption. 'They are animals, that's what they are for,' and I think she thought it was crazy that Jack even wasted his time talking to me.

Jack was softer. He was still doing what he was doing – breeding and killing – but there was a part of him that seemed uncomfortable with it. I was visiting once in relation to a sheep issue and I noticed several tiny cages on the ground with a hen or a rooster in each of them. I asked what that was about, and Jack told me that it was his wife. 'She likes to eat them,' he said. *She* likes to eat them? *You* don't eat them? I didn't ask.

It was even more interesting when he needed help rehoming Minnie. Do you remember Minnie, the goat across the road? You never saw her, but we heard her cry, at night especially. I didn't know where it was coming from, until Jack told us. Jack used to breed goats in the past, along with sheep, and he gave a kid – a baby goat – to this woman as a companion animal, a 'pet'. Minnie lived in the house along with a cat and a dog. The woman died, the estranged son found replacement homes for the cat and the dog but he didn't know what to do with the goat. He didn't try hard because, unlike the dog and the cat, in his mind Minnie was not a pet, she was food. 'I asked my Middle-Eastern friends who eat goat if they wanted *it* but they said it was too old and the meat would be tough,' he explicated when we met him later on as he was preparing the property for sale. He did this by throwing out virtually everything from in and around the house. For a while there, in the yard, there was only a large skip bin and Minnie. Minnie, who spent her entire life – seven years – in the company of a loving human and her feline and canine friends, suddenly found herself all alone, locked out of the house, confined to the space under the deck, with only Jack coming occasionally to bring some hay and check the water situation. Grief-stricken, she was as grumpy as hell, and rightly so.

Jack was relieved, we all were, when a home was found for her. 'I could have given it to Jim down the road who runs goats,' Jack explained, also using 'it' to refer to Minnie. 'Jim would shoot it and feed it to his dogs, *but it was a pet all its life, it lived with this woman in the house,*' he was emphasising, as if her 'pethood' elevated her somehow to a status above other farm animals, something Marcus, the son, completely missed but it was there, and strongly so, for Jack. Killing Minnie, as one would do with a 'normal' farm animal, represented a kind of betrayal that Jack wanted no part in. It remains unclear whether killing Minnie would have been an act of betrayal towards the goat or the human.

28

By no means was Jack an exception. Over the years we met others with similarly inconsistent attitudes. The shearer who came to shear you for the first few years kept thousands of sheep for commercial purposes, and a few as beloved companions. We're talking about the same species of animal, not like in Marcus's case. Marcus, like many of us, grew up in a society that views some species as food, others as pets. Emotionally, cognitively and in other relevant ways these species are completely comparable – a pig is a dog is a sheep is a human in everything that matters for wellbeing and happiness – but many humans never stop to think and change this intellectual and ethical flaw.

Perhaps keeping some sheep as commodities and others as companions is just a version of this flaw. After all, not all dogs and cats are loved. Stray dogs and cats are vilified and persecuted, many dogs and cats are used in cruel scientific experiments, many dogs are trapped in puppy farms and dog-loving humans are happily buying their pups in complete disregard to what happens to the mums, and so on. It's largely the dogs and cats with a

human 'owner' – dogs and cats who mean something to a human – who are loved and cared for in the human system.

Apparently we human individuals tend to see ourselves as good and moral: the bad stuff I do are lapses, deep down I'm a good person. Most sheep and other animals may disagree. Is it possible that small acts of kindness (such as loving one sheep while killing many others, or caring for a 'designer dog' while so many other dogs die in shelters every day) keeps this image of human goodness alive and makes us feel better about the atrocities we commit?

29

Maybe for Jack it was a matter of trust. You can't bring someone to trust you – like humans do with companion animals – and then betray them. Didn't the sheep and goats he kept as commodities also trust him to some extent? And don't some farmers make a huge thing out of just that – 'we love our animals, they have a great life, they are like pets to us' – before they send them off to slaughter? Most farmed animals actually live very miserable lives and die very violent deaths, but trust is definitely something I think about a lot in relation to you.

Like today when the shearer came. A new shearer, I had no idea what he was going to be like. Most shearers are okay for smaller sheep and most sheep are smaller than you. I've seen shearers shear Fifi with ease, the same shearers that struggled with you. You're big, heavy old boys and so far we've only had one who was able to shear you virtually without a cut. I'd be happy to pay him a fortune, but for some reason he's not coming our way anymore. The others have been adequate, but it's always rough.

One year we had a guy who does shearing demonstrations. He was going to shear you without a single cut, he said. I knew this wasn't going to happen when I saw his shoes, broken open at the front, and his pants halfway down his bum, and it didn't. Do you remember him? It's obviously not just a matter of strength, nor even simply of technique, it runs deeper, I think, as with any other profession.

I was relieved when I saw today's shearer with intact shoes and properly belted pants. 'A good start,' I thought.

I know that shearing is very stressful for you, but I also know you trust me to find shearers who are not going to hurt you. It's a fact, unfortunately, that I can't ever know if that is actually going to be the case. I can only hope, and in the end I'm just glad if all your body parts are still there and functioning, because accidents, including bad ones that leave sheep unable to walk

or even breathe, do happen. This disturbs me because I should have more confidence that you won't get hurt.

Today was fast, and brutal. The most brutal it's ever been. I'm sorry. I know you resent me, and you are right. You shouldn't have to go through this, humans shouldn't have interfered with the nature of your hair, they shouldn't have pushed you into a situation where shearing is required for your survival and wellbeing, and I should be able to find gentler shearers.

We're leaving the shearing chapter open for now, we have a whole year to think about it. If shearers weren't in such high demand we'd do job interviews. You're too old to be tossed around. Your hips, your knees, your neck, back, everything needs a softer touch. Softer each year.

30

Henry is not speaking to me. It couldn't be more obvious. When I sit under the deck with you sheltering from the rain or when

I sit on the rocks at night before I put you to bed Henry always comes to me demanding cuddles. You could stand there for hours getting your head and neck stroked. Last night you didn't come, and you didn't let me touch you when I approached you. You still don't. Will I ever regain your trust?

It's not entirely about the cuts, the physical violence, is it? I remember how weird it felt every time I cut my hair from long to short, especially in bed when I lay down on the pillow with a bare neck. I can only try to imagine what it is like when your entire body feels like that. Naked. Small. Suddenly all the warmth, protection, and commanding appearance the wool offered, gone.

You wouldn't go past the paddock gate last night as I was trying to take you for our evening walk. Did you feel vulnerable? Did he take off too much? On top of all this the forecast is changing, it was supposed to be warm today but it isn't. There's rain. Wind.

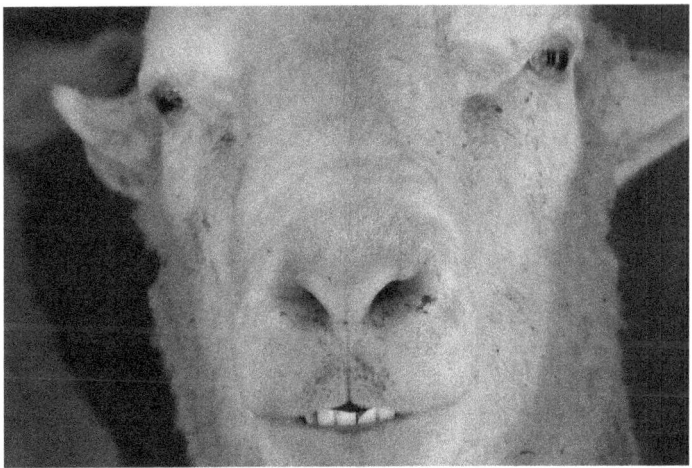

We tried to put jackets on you in the past but it didn't work. I'll fill your barn with straw and give you some more hay so you don't have to graze in the open.

Soon, hopefully, we will all feel better.

31

When sheep go through traumatic experiences together we tend to bond over those experiences.

How do you mean?

Let's say we don't know each other, and we suddenly find ourselves trapped in a pen together being shorn by that psychopath. If we survive and eventually get out of the pen and join other sheep in some big paddock somewhere, we are likely to find each other and stay together. Because now we have this thing in common – the stress and trauma – and we can talk about it, support each other, etc. Apparently humans also work that way, they also bond over meaningful experiences, good or bad.

Interesting. Humans seem to be quite similar to us, even though I often struggle to register much depth in them, but there's certainly a lot to bond over around here, good and bad.

Human scientists tested merino ewes (female sheep). They subjected them to experiences that are very stressful for sheep: transport in a trailer, being restrained, being bossed around by a working dog and being crutched (shorn around the tail and inner back legs). The ewes didn't know each other but bonded following the shared experience.

These stressors are routine procedures on farms. Relentless invasion and suffering.

It breaks my heart every time I see a truck or trailer on the highway transporting animals. Most of the time they are not going to a good place. They look scared, and rightly so. There could be a collision, they could slip and break their leg, the door could accidentally open and they could fall out – all things that do in fact happen. I try to put it out of my mind, it never really works, but there is some solace in knowing that at least for a little while they had each other, and some comfort deriving from that companionship. Then recently I saw a young bull in a rattling trailer slightly bigger than himself, attached to a battered ute racing down the highway. Torn, no doubt, from his mum and friends, heading all alone towards a complete unknown. I'll never forget his face, wide, chocolate-brown, beautiful, reflecting absolute terror.

32

Day 3. Anger.

Is it? You sounded angry this morning as you were calling out to me to accelerate *whatever-the-f-you-are-doing-in-there-baaaaaaaah* and bring you breakfast.

Anger would be in place at this stage. You were hurting and in shock the first day. The second day – yesterday – you were perhaps hurting a bit less but still in deep shock. Today you are angry. Pumpkin has been very needy – unusual for you, as if you wanted confirmation that all was still okay, that I (just) made a mistake, I didn't turn into an abusive monster. Henry is starting to feel better, I think. You're not running away from me anymore when I approach you for cuddles.

What a downpour last night! It kept me awake for a while,

I was thinking of all the sheep without shelter and of those 'fine-wool' merinos without food, being grateful that you have both: an insulated barn, an enclosed veranda, and a full tummy. I was also wondering whether to further expand the veranda, and then on my run this morning I saw someone throwing out a huge window similar to the one I utilised to enclose the eastern side. Should I get it??

Coincidentally (or not), this morning I woke from a dream in which I was discovering new rooms in houses that I knew (at least in the dream). They were beautiful houses and there was all this extra space that was all mine that I hadn't known about! Apparently it's a common dream with a variety of meanings (like all dreams). How weird that there's this shared symbolism that penetrates as deeply as dreams. The reason for my dream was probably the simple fact that I fell asleep thinking of options for your barn expansion.

I know sheep dream, as do other animals. What do you dream of? Do you ever dream of finding new rooms in your barn? Maybe *you* do. Most sheep who live in the open without a human-manufactured shelter probably don't, just like human nomads probably don't dream of rooms (they may dream of tents). Do sheep dream of huge canopies? Caves? Maybe last night you dreamt of having your wool back.

33

I wasn't aware of the connection between feed and wool quality until Helen and Ray mentioned it recently. Underfed sheep produce finer wool, and the finer the wool the more it is worth.

Humans keep sheep trapped in regions where there's nothing to eat – starved and profitable.

There's a branch of the wool industry producing what they call 'ultra-fine wool' that takes it even further: it starves sheep while also confining them to barren pens. It is also known as the battery system because it's comparable in some important ways to battery egg production. All their lives these sheep are deprived of things that you cherish most – abundance of food, being together, doing things together, going for walks, grazing, playing, basking in the sun, moon and starlight.

I love you to bits, but I also think that I'm trying to compensate for all the evil my species does to yours.

I'll build you the best veranda ever!

34

I sometimes think that if everything gets taken away from me, maybe I would be okay if I could still see stars. Not necessarily *great*, but *okay*. Do stars mean anything to you?

Many animals use stars for navigation and all sorts of other purposes, and there are places in Australia where the stars are just pure magic. Ivanhoe in central New South Wales is one such place. It was actually a photograph of snowflakes that looked like the stars in Ivanhoe that inspired the magic-detection project. The flat terrain around it and the absence of major sources of light pollution make Ivanhoe the perfect star-gazing destination. D and I used to go on road trips out that way before you came into our lives.

As a sheep you wouldn't want to be there: there's nothing to eat, humans would be coming after you, but the sky is beautiful. Whichever direction you look in Ivanhoe the horizon is filled with bright stars. If I just walk far enough I'll reach the stars! I may even reach the *Mountain Sheep in the Sky* if she doesn't run! 'Mountain sheep in the sky' is another name for Orion's Belt. Of course you won't reach her or other stars, but that's how it feels, and it's nice.

Ivanhoe is quite exceptional, but outside large cities in Australia generally stars tend to shine bright and numerous, even in regions with a relatively dense human population such as our area here. In many other parts of the world human-induced light pollution has affected the view substantially. Over eighty percent of humans (and more than ninety-nine percent of North Americans and Europeans) live under skies polluted with artificial light.[10] One third of humanity can't see the Milky Way. This may not be hugely inconvenient to humans but it can be detrimental to other animals.

Some birds rely on the Milky Way on their migratory journeys. Others use the stars for more local activities, such as finding and managing food. Harbour seals and dung beetles are among them; artificial light may seriously interfere with these processes. You'll likely never meet the seals but you see signs of the beetles all over the paddock, they are the bugs that turn your poop into little piles of soil. (As you probably knew way before we did.)

Many other animals and their habitats are also affected. Moths, bats, turtles, even wallabies! Wallabies are so-called seasonally breeding animals and they rely on the length of the day to adjust reproductive activity. Artificial lighting can interfere with this process by making days seem longer. This can alter the timing of reproduction, with potentially large-scale consequences, as in the case of sheep.

Sheep are also naturally seasonal breeders. Sheep make love and babies at a time of the year when days are shorter and nights are longer, from mid-autumn into winter. This ensures that babies are born in springtime when there's plenty of yummy, nutritious grass around that will keep mums happy and help babes grow strong and healthy.

That's why we get so randy in autumn! At least you and I do, Henry and Jonny are starting to feel a bit too old for it all.

Yep, thank goodness! Life's so peaceful now without those urges. But if the weather is right, not too warm, not too cold, not too windy, not to still, I can still get an erection over a branch with leaves attached fallen from the cherry tree.

You do, Henry! I've seen it.

Or when you rub your head into the lavender bush.

Yes, that feels nice too.

In the past I worried that perhaps you were missing girls, but then I learned that there's a lot of homosexuality in the sheep world even when girls are around and available. It made me feel better about your situation, and you do seem to love *and* like each other.

Humans have messed so much with your people! Because some humans want to eat lambs' flesh for Christmas (and all year around) farmers manipulate the breeding season and sheep end up delivering babies in winter. One in four of these babies, ten to fifteen million annually, die of starvation or exposure within forty-eight hours. If you lined up the dead bodies of the newborns head to toe, the good humans from Animal Liberation Victoria say, the line would cover more than the breadth of Australia. Imagine that!

Those who survive may develop other issues in the harsh winter conditions. For example, someone recently discovered two young sheep with feet severely affected by frostbite – a big open wound. One was literally standing on bare bone, and the farmer wasn't going to do anything other than ship them off to slaughter with the others when they all grew fat enough. Luckily they were rescued and treated.

One way of affecting the breeding season is to manipulate light conditions. The power of light, and darkness.

35

Light pollution affects humans too, but we're just starting to grasp the magnitude of it. It puts our health and wellbeing at risk – directly through the influence of artificial light on melatonin and circadian rhythms, which can lead to various health complications including cancer, and less directly, through the loss of an environmental and sensory normative, which has contributed substantially to our organic becoming and our imaginings of endings and beginnings.

Puff! We blow it all.

If sheep did something like this – systematically destroy your habitat and health – humans would say it's because you're sheep, simple creatures, you don't know better, you lack human intelligence and comprehension of complicated systems.

Human intelligence is not working very well for humans, or anyone else.

Intelligence is such a relative thing. If it's used destructively rather than constructively, what's the point? Besides, there are so many other kinds of intelligence in this world that humans know very little about. We try to compensate for our ignorance and our inadequacy by imposing our own standards onto everyone else. It always bites back.

I prefer the concept of wisdom to that of intelligence. Wisdom grows with age and experience; it has more substance. I can see it in you, and even in me.

36

The other day Little Oak Animal Sanctuary – the place you go to if we die before you – posted, on social media, the natural life expectancy for a variety of 'farmed' animals along with the age at which their life is violently ended in animal agriculture. The post, accompanied by images of three sheep elders, read:

> The chance to grow old… So many of us complain about growing older, our bodies ache, and wrinkles accumulate. Ageing is something that we should all treasure, being able to live a full life and enjoy the wisdom we acquire. For farmed animals, long life is the exception, not the rule. In fact, most animals farmed for flesh or fibre are killed whilst they are still mere babies. Did you know the following gaps between animals' natural lifespans (NL) and when they are typically slaughtered (SA = slaughter age)?

Then they gave examples: Goats: NL 12-14 years, SA 3-5 months; Pigs: NL 10-12 years, SA 5-6 months; Lambs: NL 12-14 years, SA 4-12 months; 'Beef' cattle: NL 15-20 years, SA 18 months; 'Veal' calves: NL 15-20 years; SA 1-24 weeks; Dairy cows: NL 15-20 years, SA 4 years; Hens (egg industry): NL 8 years, SA 18 months; broiler ('meat') chickens NL 8 years, SA 5-7 weeks, and others.

Twelve to fourteen years for sheep. Henry and Jonathan are at least twelve, possibly older, while Pumpkin and Jason are nine. The shearing this year was a wake-up call, it made me realise how senior you truly are, especially Henry and Jonny. Every year, every month, even every day from now on is a gift, a miracle of a kind. But isn't this always the case? One never knows when one is going to die, or how.

I'm hoping we all get a smooth, relatively peaceful death, like Charlie did. I'm also hoping you die before me.

When I die I'd like to leave no-one behind, no-one who could grieve for me or whose life and wellbeing may be jeopardised because I'm not around. The current plan is (bar some sudden illness) that when I get to a certain age I stop taking in new rescued animals, so I have no dependents. Instead I may start fostering, or move close to some good sanctuary and volunteer there on a regular basis. When I'm ready to go, I'll leave whatever there is to leave to animals, and go. I like this plan.

It's interesting to watch you age. You are getting wiser, but you're also slowing down, and Jason's brown face is starting to turn white. The trick in our situation is to make the time that you have left on this earth the best possible without turning it into a kind of gloomy hospice situation. We have

to adapt life to your changing physical circumstances but live this life fully and happily and not think about death until the day you die.

37

Let me tell you the story of a brave old lady I recently read about.

On Monday night while we were sheltering under the deck hoping the rain would stop, the beautiful humans (yes, there are some beautiful humans out there!) from Victorian Lamb Rescue were called to the rescue of an elderly sheep – later named Brooklyn – who had become 'cast', stuck on her back, like Pumpkin's mum. While poor Brooklyn was on the ground unable to get up and defend herself, ravens attacked her and pecked at her left eye. Ouch!

The eye would have to be removed surgically as soon as possible but the rescuers weren't sure Brooklyn would be able to survive general anaesthesia or cope with physical rehab after having been on the ground for a while. Were her legs strong enough? Why did she end up cast in the first place? She was old and frail, and general anaesthesia is in itself risky in sheep and other ruminants for various reasons, for example you can regurgitate and the ruminal contents can end up in your lungs and kill you.

Anyway, as it happens, once back on her legs, Brooklyn was not going to lie down again, certainly not when the humans wanted her to. She spent the entire car trip to the sanctuary standing up, a bit wobbly but onward and upward!

In the morning the vets checked her heart and decided to go ahead with surgery. The procedure went well. Once Brooklyn recovers she will go to live with a group of other elders at the sanctuary, many of whom are also lacking in the 'tooth department', just like Brooklyn is.

What do sheep without teeth eat?
Grass pellets! They eat pellets all day long!

Really?? How can we lose our teeth?

Don't be silly! I'd rather have teeth and eat everything like we do now. Besides, they don't eat dry, crunchy pellets, they eat soaked ones – you know when pellets spill onto the ground on a rainy day and turn into mush?

Yuk! I'll keep my teeth for as long as I can!

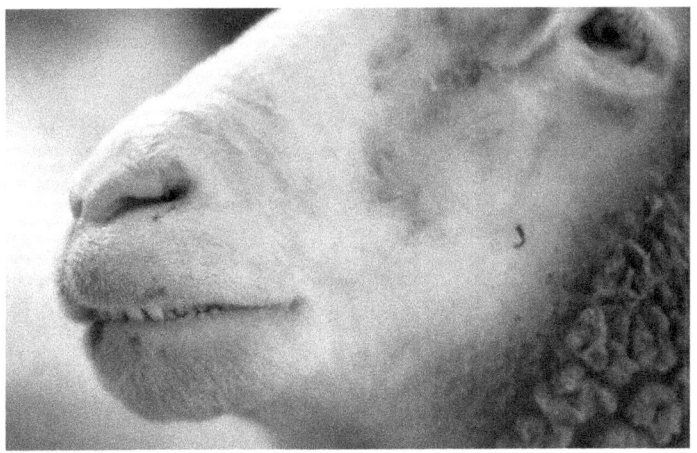

38

Sheep on farms never get old enough to lose teeth, they are slaughtered young, but generally in animal societies (sheep, human and others) elders have always played an important role. They are wiser and they also possess useful knowledge that they then pass on to the younger members. And we're back to culture.

You have culture too!

Of course we have culture!

Learning to knock on D's door wanting peanuts or cuddles was a form of culture.

It started with Jason trying to turn the knob of the door to open it but it didn't work. His mouth is somehow too small, or perhaps it is that the knob slides in his mouth the way it would slide in the grip of a greasy hand. I don't know the reason but he's never been able to complete the manoeuvre required to open the door. Relying on (the local) humans' relational decency (that is, us rushing to satisfy all your needs and greeds), he started to knock on the door, and sure enough, D opened it, once, and

then every time. The rest of you learned from Jason, marking the beginning of a cultural line. You all knock now, and D opens.

Culture. As with lots of other things, for a long time humans wanted to keep culture for ourselves. Humans always want to be *unique* in some way or another, have something that others don't have. For as long as humans don't look for a particular capacity in other animal species, we remain the only animals to possess that capacity, but as soon as we look for it in other species, there goes our uniqueness! We turn, yet again, into just another animal species, which is ultimately exactly what we are. I find this beautiful, it makes the planet feel cosy, like a giant living room full of people like me. I don't know why so many humans have a problem with it.

Anyway, by culture we mean social learning, behaviour that is passed from one individual to another and spreads across the group or across generations, and can lead to traditions. The door handle, for example. If we adopted new sheep, or if you had children, they would probably learn to knock on the door, too.

And then there is inference…

What are you doing, Henry?
 Kicking the fence.
 Why?
 So she knows that I want some of the grass that she's pulling out of the vegetable bed.
 Why do you think she'll know what you want?
 Because when I kick the door they know I want peanuts.
 I see. Do you think humans have the capacity to infer?
 I don't know, sometimes they seem to, other times they don't.

I've heard that, when in doubt, there are some good reasons to go with the more conservative option; in this case you'd assume that she doesn't understand.

That's a pretty dangerous position, that's how they judged us for a long time. I'm also pretty sure that if I followed that line I'd end up with fewer peanuts and less grass. Look! She's bringing it over.
 Well done!

39

The routes you use around here and the paths you've created as a consequence are another example of tradition and culture.

When we started to get rivers of mud flowing past the house every time it rained, eroding everything on its way, at first I felt totally overwhelmed and helpless, as one would. Then I thought of you!

You like your paths and you tend to stick to them. It's paths that you have created yourself, down a particular route, probably for a particular reason (perhaps it's the fastest way to get from A to B, or the most scenic one in sheep aesthetics, or something else…), so if I paved these paths that you've made, I reasoned, you'd likely keep using them. That was my hope, and it worked!

Some 6000 (cheaply obtained, second-hand) bricks later, laid over a period of several months by me under your close supervision, we have a path that connects all the buildings on the property and that is not only beautiful and keeps us mud-free but also functions as an excellent water disperser! I had no idea that a brick path would work that way. It absorbs the water (by capturing it through the slots between bricks) probably a lot better than those super-expensive plastic-based solutions ever would. Good old brick.

Routes tend to be a common feature in animals' cultures – fishes have routes, birds have routes – migratory pathways are essentially cultural routes. When birds are raised in captivity they don't get a chance to learn these routes from their elders. Humans have worked out that birds can be imprinted on microlight aircraft which the birds then follow and learn their migratory routes that way. An example of how human technology can help with some reparation work of the damage caused by other human technology.

40

Today is my parents' 50th wedding anniversary. I ordered them a beautifully decorated vegan cake that they'll pick up in the afternoon from their local bakery. They don't need the cake, but I guess tradition calls for one. I'll make one for us too! Funny that you like vanilla as much as I do. The vanilla sheep!

Traditions and cultures are incredibly important for all animals. Humans are becoming increasingly more aware of this. Even the United Nations are developing principles to include knowledge of animal cultures in conservation efforts. Until recently, culture was completely ignored and to a large extent this is still the case.

Humans would rescue some nonhuman animal in need, the rescuer would attend to the patient's medical needs, give them food and some shelter and then release them into 'the wild'. This is not an issue if the rescued animal is an adult and, after healing, this adult is released back into their home territory, that is, the area they were rescued from. But it *is* a major problem if we do the same with orphans raised in captivity who have zero cultural knowledge and zero knowledge of the territory into which they are being released. I sometimes think how I would manage if I had been raised by wolves or sheep, and when I got to be a young adult they'd dumped me in some human city somewhere, thinking that since I'm a human I'd know what to do in a city, speak the locals' language, know where to find food, and other things that'd help me to survive.

Too many humans still believe the myth that nonhuman animals are all driven by instinct and instinct alone, and that 'wild animals' will know what to do in the forest just because they are 'wild'. In reality, in most cases these animals don't know what to do and they die very quickly.

There is no such thing as 'the wild', it's just a human illusion. Every nook on this planet harbours vibrant communitarian living, and every animal is a complex socio-biological individual with some attributes that are inherited and many others that have to be learnt from our kin. To be able to survive and thrive, any animal – human, goat, duck, and others – needs to know the area, the people and all the other social and natural forces within it. We need to know where to find food and shelter, which predators live around and how to avoid them, we have to be careful not to breech social and moral codes when interacting with members of our own species, and so on. It takes a village to raise a child, of any species.

And as animals go about our lives and cultures we get creative, we *have to*. Creativity is another attribute that humans jealously guard as uniquely our own, but wrong we are again! My friend Carol wrote a book about it. It all makes sense. Capacities, attributes, etc., don't emerge out of nothing. Evolution uses what is there, everything is built out of and on top of existing material. This means that if we have something, in some form, other animals will have it too. The wise Mary Midgley once said: 'we can do justice to the [elephant's] trunk without pretending that nobody else has a nose.'[11] We can appreciate human culture and its specificities without pretending that other animals don't have their own.

41

One of the nice things about Facebook is that it has a memory function that reminds you of stuff you've done in the past on this day. Two years ago today, Facebook tells me, I was taking Fifi to her new home. Such a happy development, now she too can actively participate in culturing instead of being all by herself. So many things one has to learn when one joins a new community, and so much one can contribute to it, too.

Among the things one should learn really quickly in a new environment are social norms and moral codes. If you don't, the community is likely to oust you, and in most cases that's not very good for you. You know all this because you have pretty strict behavioural codes! You also know what norms I expect you to follow. Sometimes you do, other times you don't. And that's okay.

Remember when Jason broke into the feed room recently? I was in the house so I didn't see you but I'm pretty sure it was Jason because he's the only one who tries to force that door open every time I let you into the vegetable garden. There's no door knob there. It's just a matter of pushing hard enough. Once you were all inside, he came to the front and started to bleat out loud.

Come quick! They are in the feed room, they are going to eat all the hay! As you can see, I am out here and I had nothing to do with it!

That was cheeky, Jason! For a long time humans assumed (do I need to say 'Of course' again?) that humans were the only animals with social norms, everyone else lived just randomly, driven by instinct and reproductive needs. As a matter of fact, that was the official doctrine for a long time: nonhuman animal societies were believed to be driven largely by instinct, sexual/reproductive urge and aggression; all that animals did, humans believed, was fuck and fight.

This was in part because science was (and still is) patriarchal, and male humans saw what they wanted or needed to see (*why* they needed to see that way is another question…), and in part because these behaviours were more obvious and more exciting. Imagine making a documentary: you have to pack it with action to keep the viewers entertained and engaged and keep the money pouring in. Filming animals grazing peacefully and nosing each other occasionally or lying together sunbaking for hours on end wouldn't quite compare, at least in terms of what the general audience expects from the entertainment industry.

As it turns out, other than human animals also have complex

societies, in which it's actually cooperation, rather than aggression, that is more common. Having fights is costly: you can get hurt, you can even die. Having fights is stupid. Nonhuman animals have worked this out a long time ago. It's collaboration, being nice, being kind to others, helping them, listening to them, giving them space (OK, teasing them occasionally as you do with each other), that leads to prosperous individuals, communities and inter-communities relations.

Social norms and codes, which are both helpful and necessary, in reality are just an extension of how our beautiful animal brain works. Humans are funny, we tend to forget that without our animal brain and our animal body there would be no human the way we know it, and the way we feel it, love it, sometimes perhaps hate it, nurture it, see it being born, grow and die.

Everything that humans think and feel is possible not *despite* the fact that we are animals, but *because* we are animals. Because we are like you – the sheep of this world, the bears, the fishes, the birds, and others. I find this doesn't take any magic away, on the contrary, this in itself *is* pure magic.

42

Did humans really believe that we can't feel and think, that we don't learn, don't have rituals, traditions, codes of conduct and all this other stuff that we have and do?
 Some did, some didn't.
 Yes, apparently there's more to the story.

At the beginning of the 20th century some human scientists started a new field called ethology, which means the scientific study of nonhuman animal behaviour. They wanted to study other animals in their natural environment, not in artificial conditions such as labs. The purpose was to learn as much as possible about other animals, your lives and relations, and to dispel some ugly myths from the past that depicted animals as mere reflections of human vices and virtues – for example, evil snake or dumb sheep. Basically, they wanted to work out who you truly are.

In order to do so, they decided that they were going to only watch you and your behaviour, they weren't going to try to guess what you thought or what you felt. This of course doesn't mean that the early ethologists thought that you *didn't* think or feel, they just wanted to focus on what they could observe, and write about that.

Fair enough. It's a good start. But what happened over the years is that this simple guideline, which was supposed to make ethology and human knowledge of other animals more objective, turned into a strict rule and eventually into an ideology. Scientists weren't only discouraged from guessing how you feel, they were prohibited to even think, let alone mention, that you might be feeling anything. People could literally not be able to get a job in relevant areas if they were accused of the sin of 'anthropomorphism.' Anthropomorphism means attributing human-like characteristics to gods, nonhuman animals and other nonhumans. In effect, in the scientific and philosophical circles of most of the 20th century, anthropomorphism was synonymous with animal consciousness and sentience. Humans couldn't talk about nonhuman animals being sentient and having subjective lives because it wasn't something one does in that society. Most researchers conformed, letting nonhuman animals down, in fact, betraying you.

Some stood tall and didn't succumb to peer pressure. As it happens, if you wait long enough, others start to follow, and then more of them. What a relief it must have been for many to at last be able to publicly acknowledge what they had known all along: yes, animals feel and think.

43

In the 1990s things took off. The USA president at the time declared the 1990s as the 'decade of the brain'. This led to a substantial increase in brain research and the development of new technologies. It was a sad thing in many ways because so many nonhuman animals suffered and died in this research. But what came out of it was the realisation that animal brains across species are pretty similar. Even when the brains look quite different, we keep discovering parts and processes that will perform similar functions. For example, the term birdbrain, used to refer to someone that is deemed of inferior wit, comes from the erroneous belief that birds are less intelligent compared to mammals because of these brain differences. What we've discovered is that birds have other structures that do the same job, and that birds generally are really quite smart.

But you can question the wit of the human who still uses the term!

That magpie, whom D calls Sam, he's pretty smart but I wish he didn't bring us worms when he wants to be friendly.

Yuk! Did you see the other day when D's grandkids were here and Sam dumped a bunch of worms right in the middle of the table when they were having lunch?

Yes, that was soooo funny! The kids were screaming, Sam looked pretty shocked. I wonder if he's learnt that that's not appropriate.

Could we teach him to get us some peaches from up in the tree?

That's an idea!

44

The brain is a fascinating organ, it makes it all possible. The brain can sometimes mess with our lives, and that's a nuisance, but ultimately the brain is there to help us navigate in this wonderworld of entanglements and relations. One way the brain helps us in life is through its automatic categorisation system that grows and moulds through experience – for you, for me, and all other animals.

Gentle on my mind…
 Tatataaatatataaa-aaa-aa…
 I haven't heard that one in a long time!
 I like the speedy version. It makes me want to jump and shake my head!
 Yeaaaaaa, me too!
 I was just trying to say that this conversation is getting a bit heavy.
 Oh, yes, she's good at it. I think this is her 137th attempt at simplifying this whole brain issue.

Thanks guys. That was a conversation killer.

45

All-right, let's take a walk through the forest.

We are walking past trees, stumps, stones, and other stuff, and we register them all, we are conscious of them but in a kind of automatic way; we don't have to stop at singular trees and wonder 'Oh, what is this tall thing? Is it going to move or is it going to stay there so it's safe for me to walk past it?'

The reason we don't have to do this is because our brain has already placed it into the right category: the category of a tree and everything that the concept of a tree represents to me or you. Of course a tree may represent different things to different people and in different situations.

The reason our brain can do this – put the tree in the right category – is because we've encountered trees before and we have had the opportunity to form the concept of 'tree'. That's your automatic categorisation system at work!

If, on the other hand, we have never seen a tree before and this is the first tree we've ever encountered, we may take some time to explore it – look at it closely from various angles, feel it, smell it – and/or rely on someone else to explain to us what it is, how it's used (for example, as a shelter from the rain), and so on.

This automatic categorisation is an extremely useful capacity to have because in a complex world like ours, life would be impossible if we had to stop and analyse every single thing we

closer but I have to be very careful because if I graze too close then she's likely to touch me for real and it spoils that whole wonderful virtual soul caressing.

I feel the same! And then sometimes she hates what she's reading and it's like one of those creepy so-called music styles with all the squeaks and creaks and cracks… Ouch!!

You're grazing right beside me! Maybe I'm closer to getting it right. You always graze really close when something is right with the text, or if I perceive it that way.

46

There's a problem with the categorisation system, too. I'm glad I can't tell you about it because I think it would hurt you.

Given that the system offers the best possible hypothesis based on experience and acquired knowledge, it often makes us see what we expect and know, and this can lead to prejudice. For example, if a human grows up in a society that teaches that sheep are stupid and that you are just 'food & fibre', this human's categorisation system is likely to shape accordingly. So when the human meets a sheep, the human won't see the individual in front of them in all their complexity, but is more likely to just see an animal that perhaps is cute but ultimately 'it' is there to be eaten or shorn for sweaters.

Humans acquire these concepts and value orientations at a very young age, before we are capable of any serious evaluation of what we are being taught. The problem is that as adults we rarely question and fact-check our thoughts and beliefs. If we do – and encounter. Imagine that! Closely inspecting every tree and every other thing on the way. You'd never get to the grass on the other side of the forest.

So, the role of this system is to break up the complexity of life and remould it into a simplified version. This will, by necessity, be a depleted version of reality: for example, you know you are walking past a tree, but you may not know how many branches the tree has, how tall it is, perhaps even what type of tree it is. But at the same time, it is a *functional* version of reality.

All animals benefit from a certain level of order and organisation, with things neatly packed in little drawers, little categories. The world starts to make sense, it becomes more manageable, predictable, and as such, it also feels safer.

This is how we process all subjects, objects, ideas, situations, and everything else in life. Once they sit firmly in a category we talk about 'cognitive closure': the previous state of uncertainty – the state of not knowing what something is, what to do with it, and so on – has reached closure, has been resolved.

Social norms and moral codes are an extension of this system. In relationships you also need to know where things stand, how they connect, what are the likely results of a particular action, how to avoid negative consequences and increase potential for positive ones. All relations and situations are distinct and complex, but all animal societies (human, sheep, and others) work out some basic, simplified rules to follow to enable communal living.

She looks pleased, and her voice is soft and runs smoothly.

Isn't it funny how easy it is to tell from her voice, when she reads to us, whether she likes something or not?

Yes! When she likes it, it's really pleasant to listen to it, it's like my soul gets a nice long gentle scratch! And so I want to move closer and those of us who have done it – we find a completely different version of (simplified) reality. But many don't, so we end up with adult humans who tend to consider themselves completely rational yet they will, against evidence and good judgement, continue to sort animals into different categories – some will be placed into the pet category, others into the food category or some other category of use and abuse. Yet we are talking about animal species (dogs, sheep, cows, pigs…) who are sentient and completely comparable biologically, psychologically and in all sorts of other ways.

I too grew up in a society that considered humans superior and all other animals inferior. I grew up eating animal flesh and secretions such as milk and eggs, until one day it clicked! OMG! I'm causing all this suffering for absolutely no reason! So I stopped immediately.

I'm so glad I did! What a blind and miserable existence I'd have lived as a human, separated from all other beautiful animal persons populating this world, anxious at every step that my status of superiority would crumble next time a monkey, a sheep, a bee, or someone else does something amazing that challenges human uniqueness yet again. Following that life, I would also never have met you!

47

Without you I probably wouldn't spend as much time outside as I do now: sometimes doing something – building stuff, repairing stuff, planting – other times doing nothing, just sitting there, feeling the air, the smells, the sounds, awe. Awe. Awe sounds so very human but in reality, just like everything else, awe is a product of our animal brain.

I read about it, and then one day it hit me. It was in late 2013. I was sitting in the paddock, you were grazing around me, and I found myself thinking of your automatic categorisation system. It was extremely efficient! There were many stimuli coming from all sorts of directions – sounds from the road, the neighbours, the rustling tree branches, smells, many smells, including those that I couldn't detect but you could, birds flying over your head, lots of stimuli on the ground itself: duck poop among the grass, slugs, bees, twigs and others – and you so smoothly navigated through them all. Occasionally something would break this automatism and you'd pay due attention for a few seconds, and once you established that it was safe, you kept on grazing.

I thought: Is it possible that you – sheep and other animals – also encounter stuff that resists categorisation? Do you come across things that your brain can't immediately assimilate into a known template, quickly store into a little drawer in there?

The reason this is an interesting question is that the experience of awe in humans is believed to occur when we encounter something – a phenomenon or event – that our brain can't automatically categorise, it can't squeeze it into a known pattern and bring about closure. This happens not necessarily because the phenomenon or event is not familiar, it could just be perceived as too broad (psychologically speaking) to fit into anything simplified and with limits, which is ultimately what the categorisation process does.

This momentary state of uncertainty – while the brain is experiencing an encounter holistically but hasn't grasped it and it doesn't yet 'own' it – can give rise to the feeling of awe. We get pulled into this encounter, let it take over our entire being, and we keep merging and merging until we are one.

Can sheep have this kind of experiences? I believe so.

48

An insight into animal spiritual relating. In a less obvious way, this process is happening constantly in our lives. As we go about life, we touch things and are touched by them. The soft breeze brushing our cheeks, a velvety leaf between fingers, the scent of rosemary – a sheep favourite – reaching our nostrils; these are all micro-awe events that will, cumulatively, influence how we are in this world, how we feel in it – happy, unhappy, relaxed, stressed, detached, connected – and as a consequence also how we act towards it.

Wake up, Henry!

What-what? What's happening?

Nothing, just a false alarm. But you shouldn't be sleeping so soundly, it's very un-sheep-like.

And dangerous!

That's why I have you guys. Old sheep need more sleep, young sheep should stay up on guard.

No, it's the other way around, young sheep need more sleep to retain energy. You old fat guys have plenty in store!

Do you know that humans sleep all through the night?

Really? Not in bouts throughout the day like we do?

No, when they turn the lights off in the evening they go to sleep and don't get up until the morning.

How do you know that?

Because I stayed in the house with them when I was little. They put me in a pen in T's study and I stayed there all night. It was quite cosy. When I grew a bit I was able to jump the fence but I normally didn't until they got up.

What a good boy!

Goobo! Goobo!

Stop it, idiot!

Anyway, try not to wake me up if it's not serious. I was dreaming of a rosemary bush in the vegetable garden. I so wanted to rub my head into it! So I broke into the garden but the rosemary wasn't there anymore.

That's because you killed it last time you rubbed your head into it!

Oh, did I?

49

Today is very quiet. When humans come to visit they are always surprised to encounter such quietness. It's not always quiet. Sometimes everyone around us is mowing, other times subcontractors come to trim the branches around electricity lines, then someone will be chain-sawing firewood, or there are other things that can substantially disrupt the silence, but generally speaking yes, compared to many other places, it's pretty peaceful here.

I read a news article earlier and I can't get the poor roosters out of my head. Those weren't happy roosters like the ones we hear around here in the morning. Those were roosters enslaved and forced to fight each other for human pleasure.

Not that those humans get much pleasure out of it, it's really just damage causing more damage, as it happens, wounds opening up new wounds. Hurt people are more likely to hurt.

They drown their pain in alcohol, drugs and deafening music. The poor roosters are caught in the middle of it, themselves in pain and stir-crazy from the noise coming from loudspeakers and yelling humans. The one thing roosters don't have is access to drugs that could help them numb some of the misery.

Imagine what it is like to live like that, a complete antipode to the tranquillity and the softness that we have here. How can the world ever become a kinder place with so much sorrow and excess everywhere?

50

Sheep and other animals do drugs too. I wonder whether you get a chance to find anything of that kind here. I remember Pumpkin once eating from a bush down in the forest that you wouldn't normally touch. Were you self-medicating? Or getting high? Sheep do that too!

Bighorn sheep, for example, love to get stoned on lichen! They can get so addicted to it that they will break their teeth trying to scrape it off the rocks. We have a lot of lichen on the trees around here but I've never seen you eating it. Maybe it's a different kind of lichen, or maybe the real reason bighorns eat lichen is not to get high but to get the minerals from the rocks. Lichen apparently 'eats' into the rock, crumbling it and releasing minerals within. You don't need that because I buy you a mineral block. Handy, ha! And you keep your teeth intact.

Sheep (as well as wallabies) have also been spotted getting high on opium poppies. Then there's jaguars consuming ayahuasca vines. Luckily jaguars live in the Amazon (you wouldn't want to meet a jaguar!) though apparently after eating this plant they turn really soft and cuddly. Cows and horses like locoweed. Loco in Spanish means crazy. Locoweed is very toxic and you can end up with permanent neurological damage. You become disoriented, you can't find food or don't know how to use it anymore – sounds quite freaky actually.

The saddest thing is that sometimes cows, sheep and other animals can be trapped in a paddock where there is literally nothing else left to eat other than poisonous plants. When animals are not self-medicating or using them as recreational drugs, these plants would taste revolting but out of desperation they may end up eating them anyway, and die.

Animals also use medicinal plants for more directly therapeutic purposes, not just to get high: to heal after an injury, to kill worms or bacteria, aid digestion, and so on, and also as preventive measures. For example, if the monarch butterfly is infested by parasites she will lay her eggs in milkweed because milkweed is anti-parasitic and will protect her children from parasites. Isn't it fascinating?

Some of these choices are intuitive, others will be cultural – learnt and adopted from the elders. Lambs, for example, learn a lot from their mothers and other more experienced companions. Lambs eat the food they see their mothers eat, and their own children will do the same, establishing cross-generational cultural lines. In natural conditions, outside human interference, the food that mum sheep eats will be good and nutritious, enabling the lamb to grow into a healthy and happy adult. If the lamb does eat something that makes her unwell, mum will be able to guide her to a healing plant, or *used to* be able to. As humans continue to pollute and deplete the world, disease in nature spreads, while medicine shrinks.

Humans tend to forget, or simply don't know, that many pharmaceutical drugs are derived from medicinal plants. Experts estimate that by destroying the planet at the rate we are doing, we are losing one potential major drug every two years. Of course the loss is not limited to the human population, it affects all other animals as well.

51

When you graze you look mesmerised. Sometimes I call you and you're completely oblivious to it, as if you were sedated. You spend a lot more time eating than we do. I wonder if eating *feels* different to you than it does to us. How many smells and flavours do you perceive and relish or avoid?

It looks easy to browse the paddock chopping grass between the teeth on your bottom front jaw and the toothless pad on your top front jaw, but I bet it's far more complex than we imagine. I often wonder how you avoid eating insects along with the grass. I'm pretty sure you do avoid them because when I try to feed you something with an insect on it that I hadn't noticed, you refuse it – like yesterday when I gave Pumpkin a rose. 'What's wrong with it?' I thought, 'it's a favourite treat!' And out climbed a bug. Did you see it or did you hear it? Maybe you smelt it?

Also, grass too is not just grass, there is grass and there is grass. Then there is diurnal variation – what is good in the morning is perhaps not as good in the evening; I've heard that sheep generally prefer clover in the morning and grass in the evening, do you? And there's also seasonal variation.

It may all look green and more of the same to a human but not to a sheep!

Perhaps part of the reason you look so transfixed when you graze is because you feel safe. I hope you do, we've worked hard constructing a wall of protective vegetation all around us. Many sheep are confined to open paddocks with little topographical variety. They spend a lot more time being vigilant because they feel unsafe.

52

One day I will capture on video the tender moments between Pumpkin and Jason. I've tried many times but it's usually over before I get the camera out, and, when I do manage to get it out in time, the filming tends to disrupt your intimate exchange. As a consequence, the world may only imagine but never see your faces coming close together as your nostrils work visibly, absorbing scents that I cannot detect, let alone decipher, and your tongues brushing the air at each other's shoulders or sometimes touching them. Pumpkin then emits a low-pitched rumble, typical of sheep courting behaviour, followed by a gentle butting of the heads. That's the usual process, sometimes things get a bit out of hand, or hoof, as they did tonight:

There was a cherry leaf on Jason's back that Pumpkin spotted but you, Jason, knew nothing about. Pump reached across your back with his head and tried to get the leaf with his tongue. You understood this as a sexual move. You butted him vigorously, he butted back, and the whole thing, which arose out of a simple misunderstanding, turned into quite a display – a sweet display.

When you were done, I took the leaf and gave it to Pump.

Rituals. Sheep are big on rituals. I've read that if a ram tries to mount without prior courting he is always rejected.

2023

53

I think Jonathan is dying. I don't know what from. We thought it was arthritis but he's deteriorated so quickly! When I saw you on the ground, Jonny, unable to get up, with a wound above your eye and a cut in your leg – both probably a consequence of your struggle to get up – I felt anything but optimistic.

Everyone is upset. Henry in particular. He was the one to alert me that something was not right. His bleating is faint these days, a result of old age. It happens to humans too. The muscles may weaken, the mucous membranes thin or connecting tissues stiffen, affecting pitch, volume and endurance. His hearing is going too. The rest of him is as youthful as it's ever been.

Henry has always been the more outgoing one, quick to connect with other animals – humans, dogs, sheep – while you Jonny have always been shy, not quite knowing how to go about relations, either too pushy or too withdrawn, unable to quite strike the right balance, and others have responded accordingly. Despite this, I think Henry has always perceived you as his security base. In a precarious situation he'd always hide behind you. When I first saw it I thought it was funny: the big boisterous ram hiding behind a shy wether.

Once we got you up, Henry continued to bleat, faintly but persistently: he looked at me and bleated, then he turned to you and bleated at you, then back at me. I think he's realising what's happening and he doesn't want it to happen.

54

You've been standing on your feet all evening, Henry. Is this in solidarity with Jonny? Jonny is probably not going to lie down until his legs give in because he's afraid he won't be able to get up. You probably know this better than I do. But you can't stand up all night yourself. I'm worried about you. Are you going to cope if he dies? Or are you going to develop what they call 'complicated grief' and follow soon after? It's not uncommon for animals – humans, sheep and other animals – to die of grief, especially when we lose someone we've lived with all our lives – like you have with Jonny – and whom we are deeply bonded to.

55

We've been brainstorming. When it comes to sheep you can't rely on vets alone. Some vets work with sanctuaries and they'll have more experience and pressure to expand their knowledge but generally speaking large animal vets – with the exception perhaps of those specialising in horses – are not in high demand and as a result quality may be affected.

I'm starting to think that Jonny has bone cancer. I came across an interesting article that explains a recent discovery in antler and horn formation. Researchers found that genes usually responsible for tumour growth aid antler growth, so antler and horn growth are more like the growth of bone cancer than normal bones. Amazing. Of course the body regulates this process in such a way that it doesn't end up as cancer. But what if something has gone wrong with the regulation of this process in Jonathan's body? His hooves have expanded a lot over the past year, and all those bony spurs he has on his knees, his heels, even on his ears, could they be a sign of bone cancer?

The University vet made it sound super complicated to diagnose bone cancer so we've decided to try other things first. But what are those things we should try? Sy, Pumpkin's rescuer, who's now working as a small animal vet in L.A., says blood tests are unreliable in cancer detection.

56

Katy has been busy brainstorming, too. She's come up with some interesting ideas and discoveries. This morning she sent a link to a Western Australia DPI website that discusses arthritis in sheep. It reads like a horror movie script. There's the 'basic' forms of aggression that we think of when the violent industry of wool production comes to mind (such as mulesing, starvation, freezing from the cold after being shorn in winter, burning under the scorching sun in summer because there's no shade or shelter, etc.) and then there's the rest – the side effects, which tend to slip through the cracks of memory and thought.

I always associated arthritis with old subjects. Who would have thought that young sheep are most at risk? The reason for this, the website advises, is that arthritis in sheep is a result of bacterial infection, and both mulesing and shearing substantially increase the risk of such infection.

Mulesing, clearly, because it leaves poor little lambs with a huge open wound. The risk increases when the mother does what mums do best: when mum licks her baby's wound in an attempt to alleviate the pain and offer emotional support to the most important person in her life, chances of infection increase.

Shearing because most shearers are not competent enough to execute the procedure without cuts.

And other instances when the skin is broken or wet:

Ear-marking (I remember when Jason was ear-marked. Despite our begging, the pound would not release you to us without ear-tagging you first. Such a violent act. Your body cringed and twisted in pain.)

Tailing (cutting the tail off)

Castration (cutting, biting off or crushing the testicles) Ouch! It must hurt like hell.

Dog bites (I hadn't thought of dog bites, but of course working dogs may bite, clearly often enough to be included as a common cause of infection. And there are wild dogs, and packs of dogs, as

there have been around here.)

Dehorning.

The pain that lambs suffer just out of the womb. How do their tiny, gentle bodies even survive?

57

It's easy to downplay sheep pain because you don't vocalise when you are hurt physically. You vocalise when in emotional, psychological pain, you also vocalise when you are not in serious emotional pain, just annoyed with me – when I'm late with breakfast, for example, or when I buy the wrong hay. (You are so spoilt, and that's totally fine.) But you never vocalise when in physical pain. This is not unusual for prey species. Crying out would alert predators to the fact that you are hurt and vulnerable, but of course, absence of vocalisation doesn't equal absence of pain.

Sheep suffer tremendously on farms and it's all legal. It's legal to inflict such pain but it's becoming increasingly *illegal* to inform the public about it. Various countries and states around the world have introduced more or less explicit laws that allow for the prosecution of humans who dare to expose the cruelty of the animal industrial complex. Essentially, one can torture a sheep (or other 'farm' animals) without legal consequences but one can go to jail if they expose the torture, or if they rescue the tortured sheep.

The reason this is possible is because the public is fine with it, they don't really want to be confronted with graphic images on their way to the restaurant or shop.

58

Have I ever told you about mirror neurons? They are amazing. You have them, I have them, but they were first discovered in macaque monkeys, then many years later also in humans and then other animals. Essentially, they are brain cells that activate when one is doing something but also when one is watching someone else doing it. For example, when you bite into a lemon, you'll find it so sour that your face will go all weird. If someone is watching you, they are going to feel the sourness that you are feeling and their face is also likely to react accordingly, even though they are *not* themselves experiencing a real lemon in their mouth.

So when we show humans footage of the violence that is

endemic to farms and slaughterhouses, their mirror neurons fire. This makes them cringe, cry, look away; they may get angry at the activists for showing it, or they may get angry because *no one is doing anything, someone should do something*, often not realising that THEY are that *someone* who can – and should – do *something*. In any case, they react the way they do not because they care about *you* – most don't, they'll happily eat you, they'd just prefer the killing done more 'humanely' – but because it hurts *them*.

It's a good start, any start is better than no start, but only a fraction of these humans are going to go off and process it through their cognitive apparatus – the stuff that humans are supposed to excel at compared to other species: rational thinking, evaluation and decision making. These humans are then likely to turn vegan, realising that while no-one can be a perfect vegan (because there will always be some animal that will suffer just because I am alive and need a home and clothes and infrastructure, even if I don't directly pay to support their suffering and execution), it is still better to make a commitment towards the least violence, the least harm. The necessary first step toward this is abstaining from products that couldn't be produced without enslaving other sentient beings and taking complete control over their lives and deaths.

The rest of the humans are going to run away and try to get the footage out of their system as quickly as possible so they can continue their lives and eating habits undisrupted. They will still see themselves as good people, they will claim to care about other animals, they will tell you about their dog or even about how they rescue flies from spider webs. They will try to help someone in trouble if they come across them, because their mirror neurons fire and it hurts *not to* help.

When it's just one's mirror system acting up, that is, when one leaves it up to their mirror neurons to do the 'ethical work', can we truly speak of ethics or morality?

59

I sometimes wonder: Is that all there is to human ethics? Mirror neurons, fear and avoidance of pain? I think that's a big part of it. Then there's social pressure: we're conditioned to think, feel and behave the way others do. To some extent, at least when we are young, this is out of our control. Remember the categorisation system? And how we learn to see others as equal or not, worthy of consideration or not?

Humans acquire these concepts and value orientations at a very young age, before we are capable of any serious evaluation of what we are being fed – materially (meat or beans?) and ideologically (is that animal pet or food?). If we grow up eating animals, or certain species of animals, we will likely see flesh eating as 'normal' and 'natural'. I did that for the first twenty-something years of my life before I realised how much suffering my dietary habits were causing. I didn't need to be forever stuck with old templates that went against my sense of ethics and justice. No-one does. We can make different choices, and with this, we can make a difference.

Flesh eating is neither normal nor natural, it's just a consequence of humans growing up in a certain group with certain eating habits. Other groups have other habits. All through history there have been human groups and individuals who lived on a plant-based diet and did not eat other animals: think of Pythagoras and many other Ancient Greek wise men and women, various streams of Buddhism, the powerful 19th century vegetarian movement here and in the rest of the western world, and so on. A plant-based diet is easy, delicious, cheaper, better for the environment, more ethical, and even healthier.

The problem is that humans can become attached to acquired concepts and templates. They can become attached to eating the flesh of other animals not because it's the flesh of other animals, they don't even think about that part, but because they are used to it and because their beloved Nanny cooked them chicken soup or they have fond memories of helping Daddy on the BBQ on Sunday afternoons. It's the habit and/or the

occasion that they treasure – the time with Nan and Dad – more than the food itself. Fortunately, the food is easy to replace, we save lives and get to keep the memories.

But humans are far from being the all-rational creatures we like to think of ourselves as. Deep down we are little kids, fuelled in large part by habits and emotions. This can help some ignore both the benefits of a plant diet and the immense suffering that goes into their steaks, their cheese, their leather bags, their woollen coats and other products of stolen, tortured and slaughtered lives.

The resistance to acknowledging facts and changing habits once we become adults and develop the capacity for thinking and reasoning that was not quite there when we were little, is an intellectual and moral failure. A failure that is never too late to redress.

60

Oh, no! She's showing this new human the poop-scooper.
I saw! They also went around to check the barn!
Ouch! She's a bit short and skinny, do you think she'll be able to carry dinner to the barn every night?
I hope so....

I think that when Ant came the other day you knew. It could have been the fact that I took her to the feed room or got her to try the blue metal poop-scooper or showed her the barn, or a combination of all of this. One thing I really wish I could explain to you is why we have to go away every year.

It's funny but after Charlie died in late 2019 and just before the pandemic hit, I made it a new year resolution to make this place really safe – raise the fences, add some extra security gates, install cctv – and leave you home alone more often, make you more independent (within the safe confines of captivity) so that when we do go away you wouldn't miss us as much. Then the pandemic happened, and during the pandemic it wasn't just that we didn't go out so often: we didn't go out at all.

We loved it, and I think you loved it too. During those two years we bonded even more, and going away now is even harder.

I think you'd be happier if the sitters spent more time with you, and in the end they'd be happier too. You don't run up to humans like a dog may, or show some other sign of wanting to connect that humans who don't know you intimately may consider 'explicit'. Without adequate experience humans are likely to miss a lot of the stuff you're trying to communicate to them. Once humans understand sheep, one can't but fall in love with you!

That was the case for Patty! Do you remember Patty who started Animal Liberation Victoria in the 1970s? One of the true loves of her life was Prince, a very handsome sheep with the kindest-looking face: he actually looked a lot like you Henry when you smile. Just the other day there was a post about them on social media with a lovely picture of the two. She was kissing his cheek and he was smiling. 'Most people have no idea about the deep magic and nobility of sheep,' the post read. So true.

61

I'm trying to think how I'd go about you if I didn't know you personally but knew everything I know about you. How would I approach you? How would I make friends with you quickly?

I'd start with food.
Oh Jonathan, you are so boring with this food obsession of yours! I like it when humans do things with us: go for walks, lower tree branches so we can eat from them, pull out the grass behind fences.
Not when they throw the ball around. Remember that idiot who did it once? It scared the shit out of me!
At least they were trying… and the ball is still better than the freaky clothes some wear!
True.

To start with I'd wear monochrome clothes, possibly black, grey, brown or dark blue. Sheep and most other animals are not comfortable with vivid colours and patterns. Research on dogs has shown that they tend to act more nervously when a human is wearing stripes, so shelter workers and volunteers should be encouraged to avoid certain patterns, especially when they are evaluating the dog's psychological state and deciding on their fate – for example, determining whether they are adoptable or they should go on death row (of course no-one should go on death row but the system is not always just).

Sheep definitely react to patterns and colours too. We learnt it the hard way, do you remember? I'm so sorry! It was a cold spring, in 2014, when you were shorn. We were worried you'd be cold without your wool. None of the stores around here had large dog coats, so we drove fifty kilometres to a pet store at the foot of the mountains. They only had striped coats left but beggars can't be choosers. We came back with three new coats (Jason wasn't with us yet) and when I tried to put them on to you, you ran. I first thought you were playing but when Henry started to climb the fence determined to get away from that monster I was holding in my hands that was going to DEVOUR you – or whatever was going on in your head, Henry – I realised it was not play, it was genuine terror.

So, definitely, monochrome clothing! Then I'd smile at you, offer you some treats. You probably wouldn't approach my hand, so I'd put the treats down on the ground and move away. You'd come to eat them, you'd be happy. The next day maybe you'd let me pat you very gently. I'd do that for a few days. Occasionally I'd pat you a bit more vigorously, then I'd try to give you some unexpected treat: for example, I'd lower a branch for you or pull out some grass from one of the plant enclosures that you can't reach by yourself, and by day five or six we should be pretty close.

This should work with most humans, but not all. Some humans spook you and you simply don't want to be around. It has nothing to do with their clothes or anything visible, it must be a matter of energies.

62

So why do you think they go? And where?
I don't know! Do you think they have other sheep somewhere?
I hope not...
They never smell of sheep. They do smell of weird stuff though!
They do! I can't place them – the smells.
I know, right?! It's like that's how they smell when they come back. It's a come-back smell that doesn't smell like anything else I've ever experienced.

The reason we have to go is a promise we once made. Twenty years ago (the anniversary is on May 10) when D and I met, and soon after started our journey together, we had no idea we'd end up on a small property in the mountains sharing our lives with you. Back then we were very urban, and I personally always envisioned myself living in some apartment in some city somewhere. When we got married two years later and I moved to Australia, we promised my parents to visit them every year. I'm an only child, not by choice, my mother had several miscarriages before and after me. This (and other things) made my parents feel a bit emotional about me. They are also growing older and more fragile.

When we are there, we just do our usual stuff – research, write, we swim every day, we eat lovely home-grown vegetables, we see friends occasionally. One friend runs a farm animal sanctuary, so I have some nonhuman friends there too – three goats, one named after me. My favourite is little Filip, I feel we have a special bond.

And we think about you a lot!

We keep in daily contact with the humans here and if there was a problem I'd be on the first flight back. I wish *you* knew that, it gives *me* comfort knowing that we have this flexibility.

Sometimes more dramatic things happen. For example, in 2017 D had a massive heart attack. That year I nearly came back alone.

Last year it was the first time that we took a week off and drove around a bit. I'm planning to do more of it this year, if all goes well. Of course, if Jonny doesn't get better we'll have to rethink our plans.

63

A friend of mine told me that she's busy with the organisation of an event for International Women's Day next month. It's a day to remember and be thankful to all those women from the past who fought for the liberties I enjoy today: owning a house, getting an education, not being someone's property, and many others.

That's what the animal rights movement is about – extending species-relevant liberties and rights to other animals, so you too can enjoy the freedom from being harmed, the freedom from being owned by someone else, the freedom to live where you want and with whom you want, raise your own children, absorb the warmth of the sun and the magic of a starlit night – freedoms that many nonhuman animals, especially captive ones, are deprived of.

Freedom. A complex word with many layers of meaning.

Freedom is, in part, the reason for my reluctance to interfere with you, Jonny. I have my ideas about what is best for you in this period, and you have yours, some of which obviously differ from mine. The medications seem to be working, which is a great relief! I was really worried you were on your way out. It's wonderful to see you walk without a limp, keeping pace with the others, but you still have trouble getting up and lying down.

I hadn't realised how difficult it was for you to lie down until

last night when I saw you attempting it, only to end up on your nose. You spend your days standing up because of the fear of not being able to get up, of being stuck on the ground – a frightening experience for all animals but for sheep as prey species in particular – but also because it's so difficult for you to lie down. You are happy to let me help you up but not down. I'm tempted to force you down because I think you really could do with a nice long sleep, but I won't; ultimately it is your body and you know it best. Instead, I'll put more cushions out for a softer fall.

Requiem and Coda

All flesh is as grass, the glory of a sheep as a grass flower. The grass withers, the flower falls

I miss him.
Me too.
I thought those humans were going to help him, not kill him.
I think they tried.
At least it looked peaceful, he just went to sleep as he was munching on his hay.
He was doing so well for a while. He grew more comfortable being stuck on the ground knowing that T would come in the morning and help him up so he got a lot more sleep but he was still in serious pain.

I thought he was going to die that day when he was sleeping in the paddock and he started to shiver and twitch.

Yes, that was scary, it went on for hours. I think T and D also thought he was going to die. They covered him with a blanket and took turns sitting with him. Then he got up and was fine again.

For a while.

I think we underestimated his condition. Were we in denial? I increased the dose of painkillers and he was happier but not happy, he was in less pain but still in a lot of pain. To keep him in a pain-free zone or a zone of really low pain he'd have had to be medicated so heavily that he'd have been asleep most of the time. Is that a life? How am I to know? We didn't want to make that decision, we wanted to give him the opportunity to own his life and his death. 'But that's the great thing about euthanasia,' Jeremy pointed out, 'it helps you free the body of torment when the body itself is resisting giving up.' It made sense.

We'll bury him tomorrow. I'll dig the grave near the lemon tree where Charlie is buried. We'll find a nice gravestone and we'll read the poem D wrote only a few days ago. D is not happy with the poem; it clearly needs some work, but I think Jonny would appreciate it.

Jonathan Dying

I tell them a friend is dying
and they are full of sympathy.
Would they still be so
if they knew he was a sheep?
I just don't know. But he is struggling,

falls and can't get up again,
stands all night for fear
of not being able to rise if he lies down,
is becoming daily more exhausted,
looks haggard, comes and stands before me
as if in some hope or belief
I might take this thing away.

My hands are empty, the strength
has gone from my legs.
I sit in my doorway and look into his eyes,
stroke the fine, short wool on his cheek
and listen to my words
drop uselessly away.

When he dies I will have lost
a dear friend, a co-author, an
idiot savant, as hungry for life
as anyone I have seen go out of it.
I don't know which is harder to watch,
the pain he is suffering
or that of my wife as she witnesses.

This poem aches out of me.

It has no conclusion.

*

Grief is an organismic response to loss. It's hard to know what the response will be until loss occurs. It depends on several factors:

the nature of the lost relationship, the bereaved animal's psychological constitution, our attachment style, circumstances of the death, availability of social support and many other factors. What it doesn't depend on is the bereaved animal's species. Whether the bereaved animal is a sheep, a human, a parrot or other, our grief is equal.

I was worried about Henry's response since you and Jonathan spent your entire life together, literally side by side for close to thirteen years. It's like losing part of yourself. But it's Pumpkin who has been most impacted by Jonny's passing, or so it seems to me when I watch you stand at the grave with a veil of deep sadness shading your beautiful face. At night you no longer sleep in places you used to, you stand around, not quite knowing what to do with yourself. I want to hold you and tell you that everything is going to be okay, but of course it may not be. Grief can kill. The brain can get stuck in an obsessive circle of longing. This starts draining life forces from the rest of the body and eventually one dies of love. Animals who live in close-knit groups, like yourselves, and who are very bonded to each other and do everything together, are particularly at risk.

I want to distract you from it. I want to introduce new activities, new treats, give you new things to do and think about, but I don't want to overwhelm you, trivialise his death or your grief, disrespect them, take away the space you need to process the saddest of all feelings.

*

It's getting easier. The walks we take at night have become less burdened by death and absence and increasingly more imbued with the magic of life and presence. The rose we planted near the grave is thriving despite the cold weather. The trees have shed their leaves to let more light and warmth through in preparation for winter. The cycles of life carry on and we can't do much about it. They steal from us but they also bring us gifts.

Postscript

We received a beautiful gift today. The flock of Ostara (Paul, Sharon and their twenty-nine woolly friends) have sponsored Ray Ray on our behalf, in loving memory of Jonathan. Ray Ray is a sheep born without eyes. She lives with her best friend and 'seeing eye buddy' Lambini, at Edgar's Mission, another magical place that many rescued 'farm' animals call home.

Last week we weren't supposed to be burying Jonathan, we were supposed to fly to Tasmania for a few days to meet the Ostara gang. The trip was also supposed to be a little celebration of the 20th anniversary of my relationship with D. What a surprise to find that Edgar's Mission is also celebrating their 20th anniversary this May!

This is Ray Ray's story, as told by her human companions:

Driving almost halfway across the country to find a safe haven for a little lamb is not something everyone would do. But that is exactly what a kind human named Alex did to save the life of little Ray Ray, a sweet little lamb who was born without eyes.

This condition, known as microphthalmia, afflicts lambs when both parents carry this recessive gene. It is characterised by either very small or absent eyes; in Ray Ray's case, her eyes are absent.

But that does not stop Ray Ray in her desire to experience the world and all of its magic. Showing courage where few would, Ray Ray loves nothing more than to jump with wanton abandon at any opportunity.

Lambini, her 'seeing eye buddy' is never far from Ray Ray's side, and he sports a bell to ensure she always knows where he is. They share a beautiful bond.

Ray Ray has now mapped out her paddock and knows where her food, water, shelter and favourite tree to rest under are. She gravitates towards the sound of human voices, and happily accepts scratches and cuddles.

Although Ray Ray cannot see, her indomitable spirit serves to ensure we stay fast to our vision that a kinder world is possible, and that the best way to help create this is to extend our kindness and compassion to the meek and the vulnerable.

The world would be a very sad place without rescuers and advocates. Grief is tough but ultimately it is a testimony of love, and love is beautiful.

Endnotes

1   James Clear, source: jamesclear.com.

2   The text of this letter was originally written for 'The Weight of Evidence', first published as a blog on www.counterpointknowledge.org and later expanded into a photographic essay to appear in *Animated Wor(l)ds*, edited by Elizabeth Tavella and Eva Spiegelhofer, UChicago OPS, forthcoming 2024.

3   Clear, ibid.

4   Schlosser, Eric. 2001. The Chain Never Stops. Mother Jones, July/August Issue, https://www.motherjones.com/politics/2001/07/dangerous-meatpacking-jobs-eric-schlosser/

5   Compa, Lance A. 2004. Blood, Sweat, and Fear: Workers' Rights in U.S. Meat and Poultry Plants. New York: Human Rights Watch, https://digitalcommons.ilr.cornell.edu/articles/331

6   Gaynor, Kaitlyn. 2018. To Avoid Humans, More Wildlife Now Work the Night Shift. *The Conversation*, 15 June, https://theconversation.com/to-avoid-humans-more-wildlife-now-work-the-night-shift-98135

7   Nikolovska, Hristina. 2023. Metaverse Statistics to Prepare You for the Future. *Bankless Times*, 17 February, https://www.banklesstimes.com/metaverse-statistics/

8   Animals Australia. 2016. Live Export Vet: Animals Were 'Cooking from the Inside.' 15 September, https://animalsaustralia.org/latest-news/lynn-simpson-a-life-live-export-stories/

9   Covey, Steven. 2013 [1989]. *The 7 habits of highly effective people: powerful lessons in personal change.* Rosetta Books, pp.89-92.

10   Falchi, Fabio et al. 2016. The new world atlas of artificial night sky brightness. *Science Advances* 2(6), https://www.science.org/doi/10.1126/sciadv.1600377

11   Midgley, Mary. 2002 [1978], *Beast and Man.* Routledge, p. 198.

Acknowledgments

My deepest gratitude to David and the sheep for making my life amazing. They join me in thanking, in alphabetical order, the numerous humans who have over the years befriended and helped us when we needed you: Helen Bergen, Monika Bojarski, Zoie Brooks, Freya Carnie, Harry Ellington, Ralph Graham, Ken and Linda Hamilton, Miu Kinson, Nynke Kooistra, Taylor McEvoy, Brian and Lynda McKeon, Katy McMurray, Ray Mjadwesch, Marilla North, Cheraya Polinski, Atlas Thorn, Christine and Jeremy Townend, Anthea Von Staerck, and those who have read, commented on and encouraged the publication of these letters: Tanja Badalič Volk, Jason Grossman, Joanna Heathen, Jeffrey M. Masson, Sharon and Paul Mclay, Debra Merskin, Gregory Tague, John Watson. A special thanks to A. Marie Houser who came up with the idea of an (originally very different) epistolary project. Many thanks also to Edgar's Mission Sanctuary for granting us permission to reproduce Ray Ray's story, as penned by Pam Ahern, and to Little Oak Sanctuary and Lamb Care Victoria for letting us use information from their social media posts.

About the Author

Teya Brooks Pribac, PhD, is a scholar and multidisciplinary artist, living in the Australian Blue Mountains with sheep and other animals. She's a research affiliate at the University of Sydney. Her latest publications include the Nautilus award winning monograph *Enter the Animal* (Sydney UP 2021) and the recipe collection *Not Just Another Vegan Cookbook* (Blue Books 2022). Personal website: www.veganoman.org.

www.ingramcontent.com/pod-product-compliance
Lightning Source LLC
Chambersburg PA
CBHW072010290426
44109CB00018B/2194